# How to Publish
# Your Own Photography Book

# How to Publish
# Your Own Photography Book

Written By Laurie Shock

Photographs by Billy Howard

Foreword by Alison Shaw

SHOCK DESIGN BOOKS

PUBLISHED BY

SHOCK DESIGN BOOKS

454 Hamilton Street, SE, #12
Atlanta, GA  30316
Twitter: @ShockDesignBook
www.ShockDesignBooks.com
www.HowtoPublishYourOwnPhotographyBook.com

2012 ©Laurie Shock. All rights reserved. No part of this
book may be reproduced in any form or by any
means without the prior written permission of the Publisher, excepting brief quotations used in conjuction with reviews that
are written specifically for inclusion in a newspaper or magazine, online or in print.

Photographs ©Alison Shaw pages vi–vii
Photograph ©Kelbi McCumber page 30
Photographs ©Suriani Photography pages 31–33
Photographs ©Eliot Dudik pages 79–81
Photographs ©Billy Howard on all other pages. All rights
reserved. His photographs on the front cover, pgs ii, vi, viii, 10,
44, 53, and 72 are ©CARE. Special thanks go to Valenda Campbell
for permission to reproduce them in this book. www.CARE.org
www.billyhoward.com

Edited by Amy Bauman

First Edition
Printed in China
Library of Congress Number 2012909677
13-Digit ISBN 978-0-9824779-4-6

This book:
Trim size: 9 5/8'' x 8 1/4''
Paper: 140gsm GoldEast Matte
Inks: CMYK 4/c process
Flexbound with gloss laminate on cover
Fonts: Requiem and Palatino Sans

*Registration and trademark symbols are used on first occurrence in the running text throughout this book.
QR codes are sometimes printed alongside URL addresses. The QR codes were omitted in some areas
due to design issues or if the URL did not easily load upon scanning the QR code. Finally, this book
contains a lot of reference material. Companies, URLs, and their accessability can change quickly. As
time passes, some resources may become outdated. The resource section on this book's website will be
updated regularly, so be sure to check that if you encounter any issues with resources in this book.*

# CONTENTS

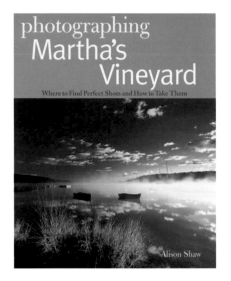

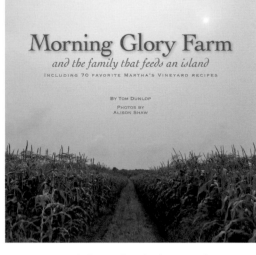

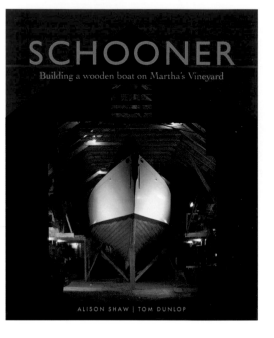

To see more of Alison Shaw's photography, books, and workshops, visit her website: www.alisonshaw.com.

# FOREWORD

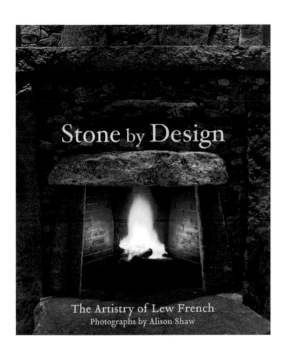

I'll never forget that moment nearly twenty years ago, standing in the dusty old newsroom at the *Vineyard Gazette*, opening a package containing an advance copy of *Vineyard Summer*, my first book of color photos. *Vineyard Summer* was printed in a small town in northern Italy, miles and worlds away from my island home. I'd hoped to be there to sign off on the printing—but realized that trip would have cost me my entire advance. The book was beautiful, just exactly as I had pictured it. The colors were lush and saturated. The production manager from Little Brown later told me how much fun the pressman had printing my book—and how proud they were of their presswork. I couldn't have been happier. I remember that pivotal moment in my career as if it had happened just yesterday.

A book of your photographs is the ultimate expression of your work. It represents a tangible milestone—one that you can share with your family, friends, and a wider audience. Even a one-person gallery show, also an important milestone, can't provide the impact of a book. A gallery show is ephemeral. While a customer might purchase a print to take home and enjoy, they're not likely to invest in the entire installation. But a book of your work is a lasting statement that will define where you are as an artist at the time it's published.

Historically, getting your own book published has been a difficult process. Happily, having a book of your photographs published is now easier than ever before—by doing it yourself.

Ten-plus years ago, you had very limited choices in book publishing. The most desirable route was to find a conventional publisher who wanted your book (no small feat), gave you an advance against royalties, and picked up all of the associated costs involved in production, marketing, and distribution. I'd be surprised if more than one in hundreds of these book proposals ever found its way to press. Today, these same publishers are struggling financially, and it's harder than ever to get them to even *look* at your book project.

At the other end of the spectrum was the option of self-publishing—at the time commonly known as vanity publishing—which did not have a particularly good reputation. The implication was that you couldn't get a conventional publisher to take your book. These books varied greatly in quality, depending on how many thousands of dollars of your own savings you were willing to spend.

In the middle ground, were art books published by universities or other small presses. While the end product might have been a beautiful book, distribution was limited, and there was little or no money in it for the photographer. Small publishers are alive and well today, but they still seem to appeal to a rarified audience.

Most of my earlier books were handled by conventional publishers, such as Random House, Little Brown, and Henry Holt. There are plusses and minuses with conventional publishing. On the up-side, it's nice to be paid for your photos, and to have someone else do all the production and distribution work. On the down-side, you are giving up control. I remember being at the print run of my first book of black-and-white photographs, *Remembrance and Light*, and watching in dismay as poorly printed pages spewed from the press. I was put in the unfortunate position of having zero say over the quality of my own book. And despite receiving a modest advance on my various books, I can guarantee you'll never get rich having your book published, regardless of what means of publishing you select; I've intentionally neglected to keep track of time spent on any given book project, since I'd rather not dwell on the fact that I'm most likely making less than minimum wage for all of my hard work.

Today, there has been a seismic shift in your ability to have a book of your photos published. The dream of publishing your own high-quality photo book is more attainable and affordable now than any time in the history of bookmaking. The doors that are now open represent far greater possibilities to choose from, with print-on-demand books being the most exciting new option for short runs of self-published books. And happily, there is no longer a stigma attached to books that you choose to publish yourself; you might be surprised to hear that most books today are actually self-published.

This is where Laurie Shock and her book, *How to Publish Your Own Photography Book*, come into the picture. It offers a complete and essential guide to publishing your photography book. Speaking from my own experiences with book publishing, the journey from a handful of photos to a completed book is rife with pitfalls, challenges, crossroads, and decisions. The world of book publishing is highly technical and esoteric in nature, and is virtually impossible to navigate without the guiding hand of someone who has been there, studied it, researched it, written about it, and taught it to countless workshop students over the years. Laurie's writing is easily accessible, and even though we've never met face-to-face, I can almost "hear" her sharing knowledge and experience with her students in a way that's fun and easy to absorb.

A high-quality book of your photos doesn't just happen—you're going to need all of the help you can get. *How to Publish Your Own Photography Book* will become your "go to" reference tool. It covers virtually everything you will need to know along the way—putting together a body of work, weighing various publishing options, financing your book, securing editing and design, printing and production, marketing and internet presence, distribution, and it includes an invaluable and exhaustive list of resources. Laurie's interviews with photographers who have published books brings some personalized and varied insights and experiences to the subject.

Laurie puts particular emphasis on what happens once you have your finished book. What good is a beautifully produced book if you fail to get it into the hands of those who will appreciate it? Selling your book should be near the top of your "to do" list, and certainly not anywhere near the bottom. Get your book into the right hands, and it can become your number one marketing tool. The publication of my first book (the one that printed so terribly) landed me a segment on *CBS Sunday Morning*, and the cover of *Nikon World* magazine. Your book can become your calling card. Produce a quality book of exceptional photographs, and doors will open.

First, read this book as inspiration. Then, once you have gathered your publishable body of work, use it again as a practical guide to make your book a reality. I'm quite certain my own copy of *How to Publish Your Own Photography Book* will be well-worn as time goes by.

— Alison Shaw

# INTRODUCTION

I began writing this book in early 2010 while teaching book-publishing seminars and workshops to photographers. I wanted something to give them to guide them in publishing their photography books after the classes were over. As I began preparing a few handouts, the various subjects expanded, the extensive resources grew, and as I neared 120 pages, I realized this was much more than a flyer on books; this was its own book. So I used print-on-demand (POD) to create a book for each student who took my class. Since that time, many photographers have approached me for copies so I decided to "personally" become part of the exciting new movement in self-publishing. A lot has happened in publishing since early 2010 so I've updated the information, added a glossary and index, and inserted a bit of my "workshop voice" to keep it as user-friendly as possible. I want people to get excited about publishing their books, to stay motivated, and not feel overwhelmed with the details. The key is being thoughtful about the process and taking it one step at a time.

Within these pages, you will find an exciting and detailed roadmap leading to your own published photography book. It may very well be a book that you've dreamed of publishing but never thought could happen. Well, it can happen, and you can do it!

Today, you can find many ways to publish a book. You'll learn about all of them here, and as you read, you'll discover which route works best for you. Is there anything I haven't covered? I'm sure there may be. But this is your journey, and my goal is to provide you with as much information as I can, in an easily accessible way. There are times when I suggest you do more research, and I guide you where to go. I offer articles to read and websites to visit, and I include an extensive resource section in the back of the book to help you with every step in the publishing and marketing process.

Like all books, there is a beginning and an end, and I'll guide you through it the entire way.

—Laurie Shock

# THE PLAN

The first step in the process of getting your photography book published is to ask yourself one very important question: "Why do I want to publish a book?"

Be honest. Is it for fame? For those royalty checks that will arrive every six months? For that solo exhibit at the International Center for Photography? If you answered "Yes" to any of these, then you will most certainly be disappointed and wonder why you went to all the trouble to publish in the first place.

If you answered:
· "For me, to expose my work, for my passion."
· "For the next leg of my journey."
· "It's part of a process."
· "Because I need to share this body of work with others,"
then there is great hope for you and your book.

As anyone involved in book publishing will tell you, they do it because they love what they do, or because they love books, or both. No one does it for the money—not publishers and not authors.

The few books that do make it big are miniscule in comparison to the total number of published titles. Getting a book published has always been one of the most difficult things to accomplish. Simply finding a publisher is daunting. There are thousands of manuscripts and brilliant bodies of work that unfortunately will never be published. However, thanks to the advances in technology and major changes in the publishing industry, there are more resources available now to help you get published than any other time in history. And even if your book never sells a million copies, there are many great reasons to publish, including exposure for your work and the many wonderful connections you will make during the process.

To be clear up front, this isn't a book about photography, what equipment to use, or how to take great photographs. This is a publishing primer, a guide to the process of weaving your images into a storytelling vehicle that will evoke emotion from your readers and transport them to an amazing new world—yours.

So let's get started.

You are a photographer, with a body of work you would like to compile and publish in book form. Within that body of work, you probably have an established running theme, several different themes, or even some overlapping themes. It's crucial at this point in the process to determine what your theme will be for the book and then choose the best images to convey the feeling and mood associated with that theme. In other words, you want to grab the attention of your readers and hold them captive. It's also wise to do some research to determine if there are other photography books for sale that have a theme similar to the one you would like to publish. If so, how is your book different? Be certain that your book will stand apart from others, or it will get lost in a sea of very similar books.

As a photographer, you naturally bring a great deal of personal emotion to each image you create. You have strong memories tied to each moment you've recorded, and therefore it's very important to have an objective person or persons help you choose which photographs to include in your book. Your readers will have no knowledge of the backstory behind that photo you took of that old tree where you would listen to your grandfather tell stories from when he traveled with the circus, or that photo of your beloved potbellied pig when the goose bit its tail—okay, maybe that last one's a keeper, but you get my drift. People viewing your work will have their own unique reactions to each image as they bring their own experiences and intimate feelings to it. The photograph needs to resonate without the personal feelings you have attached to it; it needs to stand alone and move the viewer. The person you choose to guide you in this should be someone who is knowledgeable about photography and also falls into your target market—the pool of people most likely to see and purchase your book. This may seem like a difficult part of the process, but you must step outside of yourself and be objective.

*This isn't a book about photography, what equipment to use, or how to take great photographs. This is a publishing primer, a guide to the process of weaving your images into a storytelling vehicle that will evoke emotion from your readers and transport them to an amazing new world—yours.*

Begin with a larger number of images than you think you will ultimately need. If you find later that you have to cut out some photographs, that's okay because in your final edit you will choose the very best of the best to include in the book. You may think you know now how many pages you'd like your book to be, but before you are certain of that you will need to do the following:

1. Determine the method and format in which the book will be printed and bound, because some binding methods have precise requirements.
2. Decide how much text will be included in the book; for example, you may have an introduction, acknowledgments, an essay, author bio, etc.
3. Have your text written, edited, and set in the type that the book will print in.

But don't worry about those issues just yet; they will come later.

Once you have selected a large of pool of images, you can begin the process of deciding how you will arrange them throughout the book. I'm not referring to the design of the book; I will address that later. Right now you want to focus on sequence—what image to begin with, what order works best, and whether you need to separate them into sections within the book or use the photos as one long visual narrative. Consider theme, mood, color, composition, texture, repetition of shape—how one image relates to another visually. Some photographs will work well as a pair, while you may have another that works best on a spread by itself. Remember that you're telling a story and guiding the reader through to its conclusion. You may have images that will work beautifully to transition from one part of the book to the next, but make sure that you begin and end with photographs that will leave the biggest impression and make the experience exciting and memorable. Don't rush the process. As you work, periodically walk away and live with it for a while. It's important to take your time with this part of the process.

Consider whether you want all text, including an index of captions, at the back of the book. Many times an artist will choose to have the photographs appear sans text so that the reader can experience the images without any distraction. Then at the back of the book, he or she may include an essay on the work and a list of captions following that. On the other hand, you may want to help shape the emotions and experience of your reader through text and captions explaining the photographs. It's for you to decide.

## CONVENTIONAL PUBLISHING

The Chinese invented paper making in A.D. 105. An official of the Imperial Court named Ts' ai Lun decided to try taking bark from the mulberry tree and mixing it with rags, hemp, and old fish nets to make a pulp that could then be pounded flat for writing on. This miraculous paper was shared with the world via the Silk Road and became highly desired, so much so that the Chinese kept its methods a national secret. That is until A.D. 751, when the Arabs defeated the Chinese in battle and captured prisoners who were paper-makers. The Arabs forced them to reveal their methods and created their own paper monopoly in Baghdad in A.D. 793. From there the Arabs began making the very first books with paper, which they would sew together with silk thread and bind in leather over boards. It was then that books became an industry. The Arabs revolutionized bookmaking not only in the materials used to produce them but also in adornment. They were also the first to develop a system of book reproduction. Their method, called "check reading," allowed them to make hundreds of copies where previously books were created one at a time. Some of the most beautiful books ever produced were by the Arabs during this time.

Movcable type was invented independently by the Chinese, the Koreans, and then in 1440 by Johannas Gutenberg who also invented the printing press. Steam-powered printing presses made their appearance in the early 1800s, typesetting machines in the early 1900s, and then book-manufacturing methods really didn't change much until the twentieth century with the advent of computers and software. It has been an explosion of innovation ever since.

Oh to be published by a conventional publisher! That has been the lofty dream, the be-all-end-all, the "I have arrived" ideal of so many writers and artists. While it's an exciting and wonderful feeling to attempt to share your knowledge, talent, and creativity in a form that can reach out to people who will enjoy it and share it with others, it's also very humbling to go through the actual process of approaching publishers. If you are well informed, it doesn't have to be painful. Read on.

At one time, publishing companies were profitable enough to accommodate fully staffed departments in editorial, design, and publicity. They were accessible to new talent and while having an agent to represent you was certainly desirable, one could still approach them directly with a manuscript or book concept and expect a response even if it took six to twelve months for them to get back to you. If you happened to be among the lucky few to actually land a book contract, you knew you could count on a promotions team to publicize and aggressively market your book.

I worked in the art department of one of those publishing companies from 1985–1991. Since that time, I've watched the publishing climate change dramatically; profits have dropped, entire departments have been eliminated in favor of freelance help, and the publicity staff that remain have been forced to operate on a shoestring budget. Publishers now require their authors to not only participate in the publicity and marketing of their own books—but to actually do the majority of the work.

Even with all the changes the book industry has endured, there are many great reasons to have your book chosen by a publisher—the most important of which is that they will pay for the printing, binding, and distribution of your book, and this equates to thousands of dollars.

You should be aware that many large publishers have stopped accepting unsolicited manuscript submissions altogether. The only hope of getting your foot in the door is through an agent. Abrams, the big art/photo publisher will not currently accept submissions, nor will Amphoto Books, Random House, or Simon & Schuster.

However, small independent and university presses do remain accessible and may be the best option for photography books if your theme and work fits comfortably with their publishing agenda. An agent isn't necessary to approach them and pitch your book, but be prepared to present a well-thought-out proposal as to why your book is different from others on the market and why it would sell. While I list a sampling of publishers (and agents) in the back of this book, consult the *Literary MarketPlace* (LMP) online or in print, for a comprehensive list that you can research more fully. Access the website by scanning the QR code or go to www.literarymarketplace.com. Then visit the websites of the various publishers, look for their submission requirements, and create your proposal. Don't hesitate to make submissions

*There are many great reasons to have your book chosen by a publisher—the most important of which is that they will pay for the printing, binding, and distribution of your book, and this equates to thousands of dollars.*

to several publishers at the same time but take care that your work is appropriate to their publishing agenda, which can range from any number of subjects like the natural world, preserving Hawaiian culture, the resurgence of manufacturing in the United States or preserving the stories of Appalachia. It will do you no good to send your photographic book proposal to a publisher that only produces adult fiction and romance novels. Your work should be a complementary fit to each publisher you approach, and your proposal should include an explanation of your target market, why people in that market would want to purchase your book, and a detailed plan as to how you will help market and promote it.

If you decide you still want to approach large, conventional publishers, you need to find a literary agent willing to represent you. Agents, like publishers, have submission requirements you must follow before they will consider your book. There are many different agents, and they have specific genres that they represent. Publishers and agents receive thousands of submissions from people just like you every month. One agent recently told an interviewer that he receives up to 20,000 submissions a year, and out of that he can only accept maybe five. You must stand out from all the others—you are selling yourself, make it very convincing. And remember to be patient, it may take them months before they can read your proposal and send you a response.

One of the best ways to find a good agent is by word of mouth. Ask your colleagues and friends for the name of an agent who works with photographers. If you find an agent, but he or she doesn't pitch photography books, ask for a recommendation, Chances are the agent knows a lot of other agents in the publishing industry. You can also do your own research in the *LMP* as well as in an online source called 1000 Literary Agents. Go to this website, www.1000literaryagents.com, or scan the QR code. It lists agents by geographic location and gives detailed contact information as well as the types of genres they represent.

I can make you a promise: if you do everything I tell you, put every ounce of energy you have into a proposal, work tirelessly around the clock, and follow every step letter perfect, then I promise that you will get rejection letters! It happens to everyone who puts his or her work out there. Do not be discouraged! Consider yourself part of an elite group of artists—talented and now-famous people like Sylvia Plath, Jack Kerouac, Margaret Mitchell, John Grisham, and J.K. Rowling. A rejection letter is not a measure of talent—it should light your fuse of passion to pursue your dream relentlessly. If you don't believe in your work, unconditionally, then no one else will either.

Many times it won't, but sometimes a rejection letter will come with constructive criticism. This is actually a good thing. It tells you that your work struck a chord somewhere and that an editor thought about it long enough to consider what might make it more marketable. Be sure to thank your responders for their comments and consider seriously what editors tell you. Maybe it's a fit, maybe it isn't. More often there could be a kernel of truth that you can apply to strengthen your book proposal.

Let's say that all the stars align and you do receive an offer from a publishing company. The standard procedure is that they will offer you a modest advance on the royalties you will earn from book sales. The royalties are a percentage of book sales and as a first-time author you can expect that to be somewhere between 7 and 12 percent. Make sure it is clear in the contract if the royalties will be a percentage of the list price (published price) of the book or of the price received, which is a percentage of the publisher's receipts from the booksellers. This latter number amounts to less because booksellers buy books from the publisher at a 40 to 60 percent discount off the list price. If you have offers from two or more publishers, you may have a little room to negotiate but also take into consideration the reputation and success of each publisher before you make a decision. If you have only one offer, you may not have much wiggle room, but be grateful for the interest and opportunity presented to you.

Take your time reading the contract. It should be clear that you reserve the copyright to all content, and the publisher reserves the right to publish it. The contract should specify in what language they have the right to publish it, in what form, and for how long. Is the publisher asking for fixed term publishing rights or life-of-copyright? In the U.S. your copyright lasts through your lifetime plus seventy years. If the publisher wants life-of-copyright terms, then it's wise to include a reversion clause in your publishing contract.

## REVERSION CLAUSE IN YOUR PUBLISHING CONTRACT

*This reversion clause was posted by Victoria Strauss on Writer's Beware® blog. If you don't have a fixed-term publishing contract, then a reversion clause is essential. You can customize this one to fit your book. For example, if your publisher is asking for international rights, then you would change the contract below from United States to International.*

The Work shall be considered in print if it is on sale by Publisher in any English-language edition available through normal trade channels in the United States, or if it is subject to an option or an outstanding license for any English-language edition available through normal trade channels in the United States under this Agreement. If the Work is not in print, Author may request in writing that Publisher keep the Work in print. Publisher will have six (6) months to comply. If Publisher fails to comply . . . then at the end of such six (6) month period, this Agreement shall terminate and all of the rights granted to Publisher shall revert to Author. The existence of an individual print-on-demand edition or an electronic edition shall not constitute the Work being in print unless there are total combined sales of $500 or more a year for these editions.

*Many times it won't, but sometimes a rejection letter will come with constructive criticism. This is actually a good thing. It tells you that your work struck a chord somewhere and that an editor thought about it long enough to consider what might make it more marketable. Be sure to thank them for their comments.*

Many publishers' reversion clauses simply state that the publishing rights revert back to the author once the book is out of print. But the definition of "out of print" needs to be clearly defined to protect you from a publisher retaining those rights even when your book is no longer available for sale in a physical form. So insist on a reversion clause and be sure the language is clear as to when your book is considered "out of print." Don't accept terms where they define it as "out of print in any form." Read the entire contract very carefully before signing and consult a lawyer if there is anything that is not clear to you.

In exchange for underwriting the publication of your book, the publisher reserves the right to exercise some editorial control in order to make your book more marketable. This is standard procedure, and while you are the author and certainly have some say, the publisher will want to edit the text, perhaps choose another title, maybe adjust the sequence of photographs, design the book and the jacket, and do other things of that nature. This is all part of the process, and if there is anything with which you strongly disagree, have a heart-to-heart talk with the editor assigned to your book and see what you can negotiate. As hard as it might be, try to keep emotions out of this process; it's in both of your best interests to sell your book and the editors know this business better than you do. Trust their judgement.

Be prepared to take a very active role in the marketing and promotion of your book. Your publicist will spend a great deal of time creating a buzz before the official publication date. There will be press releases, prepublication review copies, online advertising, a book blog, a website, and even a Facebook page. You will be expected to be available for travel to book-signing events, do radio interviews, speak to groups, and most likely write a blog that you have to attend to on a regular basis. This is all part of the process of getting your book exposed to your target market and building a following. You weren't shy about getting your book to this point; now you have an audience to share your talent with and to sell your books to.

## SELF-PUBLISHING

What is self-publishing, and how does one do it? This can be confusing; there are many related industry terms such as vanity publishing, subsidy publishing, book packaging, ePublishing, and print-on-demand (POD) publishing.

Simply put, self-publishing is when an author produces his or her book at his or her own expense, with full creative control and complete responsibility for printing, binding, shipping, marketing, distribution, and sales. Admittedly, this all sounds quite daunting, so let's begin examining why an author would choose to self-publish in the first place. There are many different reasons, including:

1. Author retains complete editorial and artistic control.
2. Author receives 100 percent of the profits compared with 7 to 12 percent royalties of net sales.
3. Author retains all publishing copyrights to their work.
4. Author controls the timing. Many publishers will take at least six months to review a book submission and then another year to place it into their publishing schedule.
5. Author couldn't find an agent or publisher for their book. This last one may be the most compelling reason for self-published authors!

In Bowker's Annual Book Production Report, they define nontraditional books as those coming from "the reprint/POD houses that typically use mass scanning to produce their products." It also includes "other titles printed on-demand" and records received too late to classify.

Traditional books are defined as all other newly published titles including self-published books. Bowkers also states that even POD can be used by conventional publishers to manage inventory with short runs.

Audio and ebooks are excluded.

We are in "the golden age of self-publishing!" proclaims Kelly Gallagher, vice-president of market research at Bowker® (a company that provides bibliographic information on book publishing). Self-publishing has been around for centuries, but now it's one of the fastest-growing segments of book publishing worldwide. Bowker's *Annual Book Production Report* states that in 2010, 3,806,260 nontraditional books were published, led by POD titles. That's a 368 percent increase from 2009. Following several years of unsustainable explosive growth, the 2012 report estimates the POD trend leveling off with 1,185,445 nontraditional titles published in 2011.

Very exciting information was revealed in the traditional book sector. Bowker states that 347,178 books were published in 2011, with 211,269 of those being self-published. That's a 159 percent gain from 2010! Conversely, the report shows that books by conventional publishers dropped 30 percent in 2011. Self-published books are now driving the publishing industry—a revolutionary seismic shift! Self-published books not registered with Bowker and without an ISBN, cannot be counted. Imagine what the total would be if we could include them!

Book publishing is on the cusp of a Renaissance, a rebirth of how we create and sell books to readers, as well as how people receive and read books. And self-published books, and the burgeoning methods to produce them, are playing a significant role in shaping this new world of publishing. With the explosion of all this technology, some people question the future of books. No worries there. Books aren't going anywhere. All of these exciting shifts and changes are responsible for increasing readership, which is a wonderful outcome.

In the past, self-published books have suffered a less-than-rosy reputation due to the lack of professional editing and proofreading, poor design, and substandard construction and manufacturing. People mistakenly concluded that if they simply put words or pictures on a page and had it bound, it was a quality book. As a result, reviewers, bookstores, libraries, and readers were turned off when the books didn't come close to measuring up to a professionally published book. As authors have learned from those mistakes and utilized new resources that are available, self-published books are gaining a new level of respect and competing quite well in the marketplace.

If you decide to self-publish, you will be keeping company with some very well-known authors who also chose to self-publish:

Walt Whitman: *Leaves of Grass*

Mark Twain: *Huckleberry Finn*

> (He hired salespeople to go door-to-door taking presale deposits before the book was even printed—marketing and fund-raising rolled into one!)

Irma Rombauer: *The Joy of Cooking*

> (As a housewife in St. Louis, she self-published three thousand books. It's now sold over eighteen million copies worldwide.)

Robert James Waller: *The Bridges of Madison County*

James Redfield: *The Celestine Prophecy*

*"What was once relegated to the outskirts of our industry—and even took on demeaning names like 'vanity press' is now not only a viable alternative, but what is driving the title growth of our industry today. From that standpoint, self-publishing is a true legitimate power to be reckoned with."*

—Kelly Gallager
Vice-President
Bowker Market Research
June 5, 2012

(He sold 100,000 copies from the back of his Honda. Warner Brothers eventually published the book, and it has now sold over twenty million worldwide.)

Paula Deen: *The Lady & Sons Savannah Country Cooking* and *The Lady & Sons Savannah Country Cooking 2*

And since this is a book on photography, let's list some well-known artists and photographers who have self-published their work:

Andy Warhol: *25 Cats Named Sam and One Blue Pussy*

Ed Ruscha: *Twentysix Gasoline Stations*, *Every Building on Sunset Strip*, and *Thirtyfour Parking Lots*

Hiroshi Watanabe: *Veiled Observations and Reflections*

Dennis Darling: *Desperate Pleasures*

(He gathered presale deposits for his book by offering the buyers one of four photographic prints that they would receive with the published book.)

Stephen Gill: *Coming up for Air* and *44 Photographs — Trinidad*

Richard Bickel: *The Last Great Bay — Images of Apalachicola*

Steve Parish: *The Journey*

A high-quality book and aggressive targeted marketing is what made all of these self-published books successful, and then later, many were picked up by publishing companies and sold millions. Especially with the advent of social media, books are getting more exposure to audiences than ever before—and if a viral readership develops, it can propel the book into hundreds and thousands of hands. Even editors at publishing companies have now begun lurking in the book blogs in an effort to discover the next million-dollar gem hidden among the self-published titles. Probably only one in ten thousand are chosen, but publishers are now paying closer attention.

So let's say you're thinking you'd like to self-publish your book. What method do you choose? It really depends on the type of book you want to publish and who your target market is. Keeping in mind that this is a photography book, let's go back to those confusing terms earlier in this section and determine what they mean.

VANITY PUBLISHER. This is a company that will take your book and publish it for you at your expense. A vanity publisher does not screen for quality and will publish anything. The author retains copyright, takes possession of the books, and receives all profits from any book sales. The publisher does no marketing or distribution.

SUBSIDY PUBLISHER. Authors still pay for the production of their books with these publishers, the difference is that subsidy publishers are selective about which books they publish. They will also contribute editing, proofreading, and other services to adequately prepare the book to sell—vanity publishers do not. While the author usually owns the copyright to the work, the publisher owns publishing rights as well as the books and holds possession of them until they sell, and the author receives royalty payments.

BOOK PACKAGER. Typically, a book packager plays two roles. Packagers help publishing companies, who usually don't have a large staff, produce books that the publishing company can then sell. The packager provides the writing, editing, design, layout, and even printing/binding—the publisher is then free to focus on marketing and selling. Another role some packagers play is that they conceptualize their own book ideas, produce them, and then attempt to sell them as a package to a publisher who will then market and sell them. In recent years, the role of a packager has expanded into packaging books for those who want to self-publish, whether it be an individual, a business that desires a corporate history, or a hospital needing a coffee-table book for capital campaigns and donors. Book packagers are bringing their services to those who want a book published but can't or choose not to hire their own editor, designer, and printer. In this scenario, the author pays for the service and publishing, retains all copyrights, has ownership of all books, and keeps all profits from sales. The finished books are very high quality and professionally produced in the same way publishing companies produce their own books.

## POD Companies vs. POD Publishers

*There are two main types of Print-on-Demand (POD) companies. The first includes companies like Blurb, Viovio, and MyPublisher. They charge you for the costs associated with printing and binding your book, but they are not publishing companies. You own your book and all profits associated with it. They are simply printers using the latest digital technologies to produce your book. They offer design software to help with the production of books and some even have online bookstores.*

*The second group are POD publishers and include companies like iUniverse, Xlibris, Lulu, and Createspace. They also use digital technology to print your book, but they represent themselves as book publishers who also market and distribute your book. However, in my experience, their definitions of marketing and distribution are debateable. Some may offer several publishing packages with costs ranging from hundreds to thousands of dollars. In return, you can get design, editing, and marketing services, and some pay you royalties on the sales of your book. Each has its own set of terms, so if you are leaning toward a POD publisher, do your research and determine if their services, terms, and compensation really make sense for you.*

ePUBLISHERS. These companies produce books in electronic form that can then be read in various formats on a computer, on electronic readers such as a Kindle and iPad, in Palm format, and even on smartphones. The books are created for a much smaller investment than paper-printed books, so they can be produced and placed in the market very quickly. Some ePublishers act as a conventional publisher in that if they like your book and accept it for publication, they will underwrite all costs and pay you a royalty on sales. Other companies will publish your book for a fee, and then you retain all profits. This is an exploding industry, so do your homework and compare the details of what each company has to offer.

PRINT-ON-DEMAND (POD) COMPANIES. These companies, like vanity publishers, do not screen for quality and will publish any book someone is willing to pay for. They don't use a regular printing press. Instead they digitally print very small quantities, even one copy at a time. The author visits the company's website and chooses from the template packages offered, which vary in trim size, page length, binding, and color options. For additional fees, some also have editing, design, and marketing packages to choose from and established relationships with Amazon and other sales-related venues.

The manufacturing is not of the same professional quality when compared to commercial printing and binding, and some companies will use multiple suppliers, which can result in inconsistent appearances among each book copy. One POD company, Blurb, has developed a higher-end level of books—the ProLine series. These are by far, the highest quality books I've seen in POD offerings. Look for review blogs from people who have used POD services to determine the experience and level of satisfaction provided for each company you are considering. Keep in mind, some bookstores and libraries will not accept POD books.

The fees and publishing contracts among POD companies vary greatly, so you need to compare them closely and read the fine print. Some companies will charge you for producing the book, and then you own the copyright and books. In other cases, you pay for the book, and the company takes possession of the books as well as a share of the profits.

Many have good connections with distributors as well as online bookstores. You will find a list of the most popular POD publishers in the resources section at the back of this book.

If you choose to self-publish, you may decide that you don't want to hire the services of any of these companies. You can choose to manage your own editing, design, layout, printing, binding, and shipping. This route is more time consuming and requires some education of the process, but it will save you money. In this scenario, you would be acting as the contractor, which allows you to avoid the cost mark-up that a full-service company will charge.

One very important note about self-publishing: do not attempt to do all your own editing, proofreading, layout, and design, or you risk producing a book that will not measure up to the competition. It's crucial that you have a professional editor and proofreader review your writing, even if your photography book has minimal text. Professional editors are educated and experienced in refining books and preparing them for the marketplace using the *Chicago Manual of Style*, which is the publishing standard. So unless you are a trained editor and proofreader, please trust a professional to do it for you. This is your dream book; do it right the first time. Even the best-selling writers have editors who tweak their work, and those writers treasure their editors.

It's also extremely important that the design and layout of your book be of the highest professional quality or you and your work will not be taken seriously. It is the poorly written and poorly designed books that have contributed to the bad reputation that self-published books have suffered, and you don't want to add to that. So again, unless you are a professional designer, you will need to hire a designer who is experienced with books. A logo designer, for example does not know the publishing industry or how to construct a book for printing and binding; you really need an experienced book designer. Now, if you happen to be both a photographer and a designer, then you may be able to design your book with a little education on how to structure a book and the software required to produce it. We will touch on that later in another section.

If you decide to hire out the editing, proofreading, and design, you should meet with several professionals, closely examine their client list and portfolio of work, and get detailed cost estimates from each. Pricing varies greatly by experience, geographic region, and level of quality. There are no hard-and-fast fee structures I can offer you here but I can give you some ballpark pricing of what experienced services might cost. I am using a range; however you may find that the cost estimates you receive fall outside of this range.

## EDITING AND PROOFREADING COSTS

I'm using rough hourly fees as examples here, although some editors charge by the page.

Developmental editing. This is the deepest level of editing and probably won't be necessary for minimal text in a photography book. Here the editor examines subject, sentence structure and grammar and may make changes to the substance of the text. This should occur before placing the text into a book file. This can run $40–$50 per hour.

Copyediting. This deals with spelling, grammar, accuracy, and formatting of the information and, again, occurs before the text is placed into the book design file. The cost for this can be $35–$45 per hour.

Proofreading: This happens after the text is flowed into the book file. At this stage, the editor looks at formatting within the design layout, proofs font and design consistency, cross-references page numbers listed in the table of contents and index, checks spelling, and ensures that all text complies with the *Chicago Manual of Style*. This can run $20–$35 per hour.

## DESIGN AND LAYOUT COSTS

Many book designers will provide you with a total cost estimate based on page count and complexity of the book. Per-page rates can range from $35–$75 per page with the higher end being from more experienced, talented book designers. On top of that, they will charge a book cover design fee that may range between $800 and $1,750. That fee will include case and jacket design with all finishing specifications. Designers may also have expenses for color proofs and courier/shipping costs, which they would charge back to you. If you required them to also acquire your ISBN, LC number, and barcode, those would be additional charges you would be responsible for.

Remember to look closely at your potential designers' book samples and be certain that they have actual book-design experience. If you don't care much for what you see in their samples, then you probably won't be pleased with the book they create for you.

Finally, unless you have a Heidelberg press in your basement for those pet projects on weekends, you will need to find a quality book manufacturer. There are many to choose from, and pricing and quality varies greatly, so it's important to acquire print quotes from several reputable companies. Always ask for samples of each company's books; if they do good quality work, they will be happy to send you examples. Many books are printed and bound outside of the United States because it is more cost effective to do so. Even with the shipping costs, it can save up to 35 percent depending on the quantity and type of book you are producing.

For various reasons, some people feel strongly that they only want to print here in the United States; for others, the more affordable overseas printing costs are the difference between doing the book and not doing it. I feel it's good to get pricing both domestically and overseas before making a final decision. There are companies here in the United States that produce beautiful high quality books as there are companies in Spain, Italy, Asia, Mexico, and Canada. But there are also companies who do not, so you need to understand who you are working with and the level of quality they can provide. In the resources section, I provide a list of my preferred printers and binders. If you are considering working with a company outside of my list, do your research and be sure to ask for book samples similar to the kind of book you are publishing. Don't be satisfied if all they send you are paperback novels as samples. You need to see examples of fine art photography books so that you can examine the quality of materials, binding, and construction. You can also ask to view their client list and obtain references to learn more about the experiences of others who have worked with that particular printer.

*The most important things to remember if you choose to manage the self-publishing yourself are: (1) educate yourself, and (2) utilize professional resources to make your book indistinguishable from a book produced by a publishing company.*

## Printing and Binding Costs

So you might be wondering, "If I do self-publish, what will the approximate printing, binding, and shipping costs be?" It's really hard to say because every book has a unique set of specifications: trim size, page count, number of inks, and print quantity. But just to give you an idea of pricing, here's an example of what a book printed in China would cost today (pricing in United States would be higher):

- 1,000 book print run
- hardcover smyth-sewn section binding
- 10" x 10" square trim size with 138 pages
- ink: CMYK 4/color process throughout
- paper stock: 157gsm Sun Matte
- French-fold jacket with flood matte lamination and spot UV coating
- cover finishing: debossing book title on the front cloth-covered case and foil stamp title on the spine
- shipping and residential delivery

---

$12,760  ($12.76 a copy)

If your book is a smaller size and softcover with fewer pages, then the price will be significantly less. Each book is different, so you really need to get cost estimates based on your book's unique specifications.

The most important things to remember if you choose to manage the self-publishing yourself are: (1) educate yourself, and (2) utilize professional resources to make your book indistinguishable from a book produced by a publishing company.

If you have decided to self-publish your book, it's no secret now: it's going to cost you some money. How much you need will depend on which method of self-publishing you choose.

There are several ways you can collect the funds to begin the process—you can sell off that little island you bought a few years ago and hardly visit anymore, draw down on that trust fund Great Uncle Alstorpheous and Aunt Drucilla set up for you, or cash in those shares of Apple you bought at $42 each. Or perhaps you are like most of us and need to develop a strategy to raise money. This will take a little time and planning.

First, ask yourself "Who is your target market?" Be realistic: photography books typically have niche markets; they are not for the masses. So you need to identify those markets and then look at resources related to them that might turn out to be a source of funding.

1. Are you represented by a gallery that has an extensive mailing list?

2. Is your photography environmentally themed? If so, you could approach nonprofits who might be interested in partnering/or buying a block of books for their cause.

3. Is your photography focused on a current social issue that might get the attention of an organization immersed in that same issue?

4. Could your photography be connected to a future event that could gain attention?

5. Is your work related to a specific city or region where you could find some local sponsors interested in supporting the project?

6. What grants might be available to you for this subject matter?

7. Is this a documentary book, and is it your first book? If so, there are specific grants available for those publishing their first book. See the resources section of this book.

8. Consider offering a free photographic print to people who would pay for a book in advance. Presales are a great way to raise the money you need to produce your book and create an early buzz about it. Include a patron's page at the end of the book listing the names of all who supported the book's publication.

9. Ask a local restaurant or frame shop to host an event where you can sell your prints to raise money to publish your book. You could also ask a friend to host a temporary gallery in his or her home and invite guests to view and purchase your work.

10. Approach a paper mill with a proposal to publish your work. Many times these companies are interested in a fresh way to showcase their premium printing papers. You might be able to strike a deal with them to produce your work in book form. This will publish your work and provide them with a beautiful book that they can use for their marketing.

11. Finding a hook with another organization or cause can be a great way to create a connection with someone who can help fund the publishing of your book.

12. Crowdsourced funding is the hottest new form of raising money for a creative project. My favorite company for this is Kickstarter. Submit your project concept to Kickstarter, and they determine if it fits within their guidelines. Their guidelines include things like: it can't be a charity such as buying a computer for a student or it can't be a self-help project. You set a limit on how much money you need to raise as well as a timeline for fund-raising which can be anywhere from 1 to 90 days. You must offer rewards for various levels of contributions. It might be a postcard for those who contribute $10, or a fine art print for those who contribute $500. Kickstarter posts the project on its website, and you begin telling everyone you know to make contributions on the site. Launch a major email blast, post it on Facebook, and get the word out there. As contributions roll in, Kickstarter posts your fund-raising progress. If you reach your goal before the deadline, you receive the contributions less 5 percent for Kickstarter. If you don't reach your goal before the deadline, none of the money is officially collected, and you get nothing.

*Even a prodigy must find a way for his or her book to stand out from other photography books and make it something that people will want to buy.*

It's very important to ask yourself, "What makes my photography book different from others?" and "Why would someone buy my book over another photography book of the same subject?" You must find a way for your book to stand out so that people will want to buy it over others. If you can do this, it will make it easier to find grants and/or organizations willing to help fund the project. Carefully define the purpose of your book and your audience. Then be passionate about it—believe in your book and make others believe in it, too.

## CREATING A PRODUCTION BUDGET

As you are determining how to raise the money to publish your book, you need to know how much money you have to raise. It's important that you develop a budget for the book and then monitor that budget closely as you progress. Here is a list of some items you need to include in your budget, specific to your photography book:

### HIGH-RESOLUTION SCANS OF YOUR PHOTOGRAPHS (*unless they are digital*):

A drum or professional scanner is required for this. If you do not have access to these high-end scanners, specialists exist who can do this for you. This is crucial for a photography book as the final book will be only as good as the scans you include.

### COLOR MANAGEMENT AND DIGITAL TWEAKING:

If you do not have a calibrated computer monitor, you will need professional help with color management. This is a very important step for a photography book. If the digital information is not correct, your photographs will not reproduce correctly on press. A Seattle company, iocolor, offers scanning and color management. They perform test prints on the specific press that will print your book. Then they create a custom color profile, apply it to your photographs, and generate color proofs to match for accurate printing. Most printers offer ICC color profiles, but they are generic—iocolor's are custom for your book. It can add $2,000–$3,000 to the budget, but it's worth it. Four Colour Print Group has good color management if you cannot afford the extra step that iocolor provides. Whatever company you choose, make sure you have a system in place to manage color.

### COPYEDITING AND PROOFREADING OF WRITTEN TEXT

Jacket copy
Front matter: copyright page, introduction, table of contents
Captions or photo titles
Back matter: author statement, author biography, acknowledgments

### DESIGN AND LAYOUT OF BOOK INTERIOR AND COVER

COPYRIGHT REGISTRATION

ISBN (International Standard Book Number): You need this number for your book to be included in a searchable database of Books in Print. It enables bookstores to order it for their store. You can buy a single ISBN for $125 through www.bowker.com, or you can buy a block of ten for $250.

BOOKLAND EAN BARCODE: You must have this in order for the cash register scanner to complete the book purchase. It costs about $25 and is available through Bowker and other online vendors.

COLOR LASER PROOFS OF YOUR BOOK: You will send these proofs to an editor, proofreader, and printer during the development of your book. The paper and ink costs for these proofs should be part of your budget as well.

MAILING COSTS OF BOOK PROOFS TO EDITOR, DESIGNER, AND PRINTER

PRINTING, BINDING, AND SHIPPING OF BOOKS

WAREHOUSING THE BOOKS: It must be a temperature-controlled space.

FULFILLMENT: (*If you do not have a distributor, will you fulfill orders?*): If you don't have a distributor, and you cannot store the books, there are fulfillment centers that will warehouse and process orders for your books for 20-25 percent of your book's list price. This takes a good chunk of the profits, so I try to find ways not to use them.

MARKETING PLAN: This may be required before public relations professionals and distributors will work with you. They want to see that you have a well-thought out plan to market and sell your book. You will need to do some research or hire help for this if you have never written a book-marketing plan.

COSTS RELATED TO EXECUTING THE MARKETING PLAN: This includes items such as postcards, ads, bookmarks, press kits, etc. For postcards, I like to use Modern Postcard because they are inexpensive, offer fast turnaround, and deliver great-quality cards.

PUBLICITY PLAN: It's wise to hire a publicity specialist specific to book publishing. A public relations (PR) person in New York City can cost around $5,000, but they have connections in television and radio that you do not. You can do this yourself, but you will need to be assertive and learn to prepare your own press release and media kits. In addition, I like using Lisa Roe, a social media PR person based in Milwaukee, who charges about $1,000 and can really help gain exposure and reviews on the web. I'm sure there are other specialists in your area as well.

PREPUBLICATION REVIEW COPIES: Also known as "uncorrected proofs," these are soft-bound copies of your book before the final proofreading is completed. You send them to book reviewers four months before your book is published. I like using local printers to print them digitally and perfect bind them in a short run of twenty-five to fifty copies. You could also print copies off of your color printer and have them bound at a copy store to save money. Your publicist will mail these out to reviewers around the country. But if you are doing your own publicity, you will need to add in the packaging and postage costs to mail these out.

CATERING OR SNACKS FOR BOOK SIGNINGS AND EVENTS

WEBSITE FOR THE BOOK AND A BLOG

Now that you have a list of items to budget for, you will need to begin finalizing the size and page length of your book in order to request print quotes. In those quote requests, the printer will need to know the following:

BINDING TYPE: Books are produced as hardcover or softcover. Softcover books can be spiral bound, perfect bound, side sewn, or smyth sewn. Perfect bound is not an archival binding—

this means the book will not last over time with use. The bound edges of the paper are roughed up, glue is added, and then the cover is adhered. Those pages will eventually fall out; I promise you. Side sewn is durable, but you can't open the pages flat. Smyth sewn is durable, and you can completely open the book flat. But for a photography book, a hardcover book is best, so specify a hardcover "case-bound" book that is smyth sewn. I find that if the quantity is less than ten thousand and you're printing outside the country, the price isn't significantly different between soft- and hardcover. If you prefer a softcover, you still want the sewn signatures, and you are printing in Asia, you can specify the binding as Limpbound. Four Colour Print Group produces an even nicer version of a softcover, smyth-sewn book called FlexBind.

TRIM SIZE: This is the actual page size; not the cover measurement.

NUMBER OF PAGES: Smyth-sewn books are printed in multiple pages on one sheet of paper called a signature. The paper is folded down into pages and then trimmed. Typically, books are bound in 16-page signatures, although some print with 8-, 10-, and 12-pages. Estimate your page count as a multiple of 16 or ask your printer how many signatures to plan for.

PAPER STOCK: It's subjective of course, but I feel a photography book needs a premium-coated paper stock that will hold the ink on the surface and generously reflect light. If you are going for a particular tone and feel, perhaps you want to print on a super-smooth uncoated stock for a natural, earthy feel. But 95 percent of the time, I prefer paper that isn't glossy, like a dull- or satin-coated stock. If it's in the budget, I also use a gloss varnish printed over just the photographs for pop. It makes the photographs seem as though they're floating slightly over the page itself. I also prefer heavier-weight papers; the higher the number the heavier the paper. I like to use a 100-pound sheet when printing domestically. When printing in China, 157GSM Matte Art, 157GSM Sun Matte, and 157GSM Goldeast Matte are all comparable and very nice sheets. In South Korea, I use 150GSM Matte Art or a satin version, which has a warm tone. Spain, Italy, and other countries all have their own paper suppliers. Think about the paper shade and what will work best for your photographs. Some papers are solar white, while others are warm—each will make your photographs look a little different, so pay close attention to the tone of the paper. Be sure to ask for paper samples from each printer from whom you request quotes.

INKS: Do you want a black-and-white or full color book? Even if you want black-and-white, I recommend printing the book in CMYK, 4/color process black-and-white. Your photographs will be richer and have greater depth than if printed in one color (black). If you want to save a little money, you can print 2/color, black and 1 PMS (Pantone matching system) ink. If you create duotones of your photographs, you will get a deep rich tone without the expense of 4/color. Some photographers will print their black-and-white photographs tri-tone for increased complexity of tone. If you are considering the 2/color, I suggest you compare those costs with 4/color and then decide if the money you would save is worth it.

ENDPAPERS OR ENDSHEETS: Do you want printing on the endpapers? The endpapers are the pages that are glued to the inside front and back cover of the book. You can spec these to be the same paper stock as the interior and then print a photograph or solid ink on them, or you can choose endpapers in various colors and textures; it's your choice.

JACKET AND CASE COVER: Do you want a jacket to wrap the hard case of the book? Most photography books have them, but you don't have to have one. You can forego the jacket and just have cloth with a foil stamp of the book title on the cover and spine. You can use cloth and tip-in a photograph on top of the cloth, but it may be more expensive. You can have a printed litho case, which is kind of like the printed jacket glued around the case. You can get really fancy and have a slip case or clam-shell box that the book fits into. It's just good to know that you can get creative with this. If the book is large format, say 10" x 12", 11" x 14" or larger, I like to spec a French-fold jacket. You will see them on many large photography and art books. When a book is large, a regular jacket can begin to curl up, and then it is vulnerable to rips and tears. A French-fold jacket is a larger sheet of paper that folds over, top and bottom, and then wraps around the book. It looks the same as a regular jacket unless you examine it closely. It's

### WHEN DID YOUR INTEREST IN PHOTOGRAPHY FIRST BEGIN?

I was first drawn to photography when I was in college, and actually even before that, because when I look back at old family photo albums I've noticed that I had taken a lot of the pictures, because I'm not in them.

But I studied sociology and psychology in school—at that time in the '70s that's what everybody was doing. It was all about peace and social work and social consciousness. Quite frankly I think without that background and influence, I'm not so sure I would have started doing documentaries when I became a photographer.

I eventually went back to school and took some art classes. It came time to choose electives, and I took my first photography class and I literally fell in love with it.

### WHAT WAS YOUR FIRST PROFESSIONAL PHOTOGRAPHY JOB?

My first job in photography was at Emory University in Atlanta. I was a staff photographer working on their magazine. One of the highlights for me was when Gorbachev came to Emory as the keynote speaker for graduation, and I got to follow him around. That job was important because it catapulted me to a higher level, allowed me to stretch in terms of the kind of work I did, and gave me the confidence to free-lance and work with the Atlanta Committee for the Olympic Games, *Atlanta Magazine,* and other corporate clients.

Photographer Marilyn Suriani is a documentary and fine art photographer. Her book was published by Prometheus Books and is titled, *Dancing Naked in the Material World.* To see more of Marilyn's work, visit her website: www.surianiphoto.com.

To see the full multimedia interview with Marilyn as well as interviews with other photographers, go to www.HowtoPublishYour OwnPhotographyBook.com or scan this QR code with your smartphone.

A CONVERSATION WITH *Marilyn Suriani*

**HOW DID YOU DECIDE ON THE SUBJECT MATTER FOR YOUR BOOK?**

I began building a body of work photographing strippers. It started as an assignment from my instructor, Dennis Darling, at the Portfolio Center where I was studying photography. He wanted me to do something in a sequence as part of my documentary studies.

I was fascinated with the whole idea of strippers, and I think it was because it was sort of taboo. And I was a woman, and it was like, "Why in the world would women do such a thing?" I've always been very curious so to me it was interesting.

I was able to get into a club, the Cheetah. I went in before hours and photographed a woman stripping. In my mind, it was a Gypsy Rose Lee kind of a thing, but strippers don't do Gypsy Rose Lee dances anymore, or strip-tease acts. It's now-you-see-the-clothes and now-you-don't. So I had to slow her down, but I got the shot and that was how it started.

I went to work at the Gold Club toward the end of the book. Because of Gloria Steinem and her stint at the Playboy Club, I thought it would be fun to go undercover. So, I worked as a cocktail waitress, and my first day on the job I was greeted by a waitress who was going to show me the ropes. She took me into the dressing room and said, "This is a snake system here. There are no sections; it's first come first serve."

And she wasn't kidding, They would line up at the door and wait for customers to come in and take their drink order as soon as they walked in, which I could never do.

You had to put your uniform on at the club. So I'm in the dressing room, and one of the guy managers just walks in while I'm getting dressed, and I was shocked because I realized there was absolutely no privacy. There was no respect for the women at all. The management was extremely chauvinistic and liked having the women compete with each other, because the last thing they wanted was for any of them to band together. I called it Dante's Inferno. No windows; it's the middle of the day, and it's dark, and it smells like cigarettes and alcohol. It wasn't a pleasant experience.

**WHAT DID YOU WANT TO COMMUNICATE WITH THIS BODY OF WORK?**

I learned a lot from talking to the women about how they felt about the men, the way that they were manipulated, and the way the women manipulated the men. This work was a social essay about what it's like to be a stripper. It's not a fluff piece, it's not a glamorous life, far from it. So that became the heart of the book; it's about someone who becomes a stripper, so their words were just as important as the images. The images have to be strong, but the words really enhanced the photograph. To me it was much more interesting for it to be in the words of the strippers. I could've made all kinds of comments about stripping, and what I thought about it, but it had much more appeal coming from them.

9" x 8" trim size with 132 pages
Paper stock: 100-pound dull coated
Perfect bound with hard cover case
Jacket with flood gloss laminate
Ink: duotones on jacket and interior
Conventionally published with a 3,000 book print run
Printed and bound in the United States
Photographs taken with Rolleicord, Minolta 101, and Hassalblad
List price: $39.00

**WHAT PROCESS DID YOU USE TO EDIT YOUR PHOTOGRAPHS INTO A MANAGEABLE COLLECTION FOR THE BOOK?**

That was quite difficult at first, so I asked two of my photographer friends, who I trusted to be objective, to help me with the editing. If we don't involve other people in the edit, we can get really bogged down. We get emotionally attached to an image because of the circumstance, and it doesn't always translate through the image. You may have had an emotion with that image, but you've got to look at it objectively, which is hard to do when you're attached. Your designer is the number-one person who can help you with that because they are visual in a way that we're not. They're used to designing books, they're used to putting words and books together, they know how images work on a page. I also think it's important to get support, criticism, and ideas from your peers, other photographers, a teacher, a mentor, or a curator.

### How did you go about designing your book?

After going to the Houston Photo Show, they said I needed a book mockup, between twenty and thirty pages and that I needed an outline and an introduction. At that time, I didn't have a designer so I did that on my own. I put the pages together using printed copies. My understanding was that it was the content and words that were most important because that's what the publisher is interested in, the design could be massaged.

After landing my publishing contract, I did hire a book designer.

### How did you find your publisher?

I went to some university presses first, approached several, and got turned down. Then the University of Illinois said they wanted it. They sent me a contract and had a board

meeting. The board was too scared of the subject matter and decided not to do the book.

I also worked with a couple of literary agents but they weren't able to find an interested publisher. Finally, I had a friend who knew a literary agent and he told her about my project. Upon seeing the book mockup, she loved it and agreed to represent me. Through her help, I received an offer from Prometheus Books. A lot can happen by networking with the people you know!

### How long did you work on your book before it was published?

I've never done a project that I could complete in six months. All of my projects have taken a while. It takes time to really get to know people. You really have to spend some time doing that.

The stripper project, from beginning to end, took about twelve years. I took three years off for kids, and from the time the book was contracted and it finally got published, it was probably a two-and-a-half-year period. It was a major commitment for me.

### What was your print run?

We printed and sold three thousand books. It's officially out of print now, but you can still find copies if you search online.

### Was the marketing handled by your publishing company?

Yes, Prometheus sent out a lot of press

A CONVERSATION WITH *Marilyn Suriani*

releases to magazines and to newspapers, although it was a small budget and they needed supplemental help. My agent procured my first gallery exhibition in New York. Now called the Leica Gallery, my exhibit was their very first photo show.

While I was in New York, the publisher was able to get me on the *Sally Jesse Raphael Show*. They flew up four of the strippers, one of them was Blondie and one mother and one husband. We we took over the whole show. They showed my book on TV, and they made a plug for the gallery opening.

### Did you do any of the promotions and marketing yourself?
Absolutely. I had a book signing at a local Atlanta bookstore, and I sold one hundred books. I decided to do my second book signing at the Clermont Lounge. Clermont is a blue-collar strip club, anybody can go in there and in most strip clubs you usually have to be accompanied by a man to get in, at least it used to be that way. It was even a bigger success; people were lined up outside the door.

I contacted a few publications here in the city, *Atlanta Magazine* and *Creative Loafing*. I did a radio interview with NPR, and I was on *Noon Day Atlanta*, a local television show.

### What advice can you give to other photographers who would like to publish their work?
I would say make sure you have a cohesive body of work. I wouldn't try to put everything you've photographed into one book. If there's no thread, it's just a collection of images. A book needs photographs with a common theme. And you need some guidance in producing a book; if you try to do it by yourself, you're making a big mistake.

### What are you currently working on?
I've kind of shifted over the years and am focusing on self-portraiture. For me it's about aging, it's about how the body changes, about how we live our lives day to day and most of us really have no idea what's going on inside. There's a disconnect for most of us between the interior and the exterior. I started noticing that when I turned 50 and I wanted to figure out a way to deal with my aging process and maybe, at the same time, become somewhat objective about it, if I could.

I've now begun to include other women, women of a certain age. Because I think women over 55 are one of the biggest

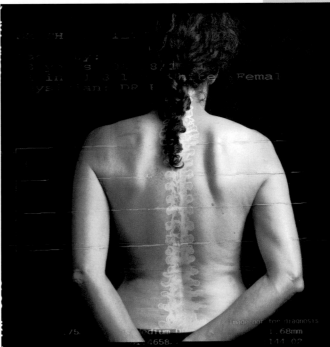

groups in the country now. We have a lot of buying power, we are living longer, and there are more of us. And we've all been so subjected to body image via magazines, television, and advertising. What I intend to do is honor women's bodies as they age but doing it from the point of view of their everyday life. So what started out as self-portrait work, is more of a portrait of women—aging women.

# The Process

If you are reading this and planning to publish a book of your photography to share with your peers, amateur and professional photographers, critics in the art community, and art lovers, then you truly want your work to be taken seriously.

You've invested a great deal of time and energy learning and growing as an artist, you've invested a significant amount of money in photographic equipment to pursue your passion, and you've created a sizable body of work that represents earnest commitment to your vision and craft.

As you enter into the process phase of publishing your book, it's imperative that you maintain that same level of presentation. You are creating an important package for your photographs—the vehicle that will introduce people to your work. This is not the time to cut corners in quality; your book will be competing with photography books produced by galleries, museums, and art publishers. This is your publishing debut, and the first impression is a lasting one.

If you have found a publisher for your book, congratulations! Chances are good you won't have to be concerned with the level of quality because they will take care of that for you. As you are shown editing changes and design layouts, if you don't agree with all of their decisions, feel free to calmly discuss it with your editor. You are partners in this endeavor, and while you may have some differing opinions on a few things, typically these should be easy to negotiate.

If you've chosen a company to manage the self-publishing of your book, hopefully you've done your due diligence by requesting book samples. These will help you ascertain the company's competence in the editing and designing of their books as well as the quality of the materials they use. Do not think that you can completely relax at this point; you need to exercise quality control throughout the process. Before you sign any contract, be sure to ask how many designs you will be shown for the agreed-upon price. Also ask how many changes you can make without incurring additional costs. Be certain you know exactly what to expect as you begin receiving materials from them.

Double check and proofread everything they send you during the process. As you are presented with designs for the cover and the interior, you need to play an active role in guiding them toward the look and feel you want. Don't be afraid to ask for revisions and changes as your contract provides. You must share your vision with them, and in time and with careful communication, you should arrive at the perfect book for your photography. It does take time though. Be patient and remember it is a process.

If you have decided to act as your own contractor in the self-publishing of your book, then it is your responsibility to find a quality editor and book designer to help you. There are many very talented editors and designers, and I find that the best way to find them is to look at other self-published books, go to the copyright page, and see if their names are listed in the production of the book. If they are not, contact the author and ask who they used and what their experience was. Word of mouth is one of the best ways to find talented and experienced—I'll say it again—*experienced* people in publishing.

Many small, local publishers will use book editors and designers on a free-lance basis. Call local publishers and ask who they use to edit, proofread, and design their books. That is a wonderful way to find experienced professionals who know what they are doing and work in publishing every day.

I cannot tell you how many times I have had a client say to me, "I don't need you to edit or proofread my book. My sister is a business professional, and she's really smart. She has looked at this ten times, and I trust her. She even has a few ideas for writing her own book," or "I don't want you to handle the editing and proofreading; my husband is a lawyer, and he can do that for me and save some money."

Red flag! Are these aforementioned people smart? Yes, I'm quite sure they are. Are they experienced book editors with knowledge of the *Chicago Manual of Style* and how to edit a book for publication? No, I can make a pretty good guess that they are not.

*Before you sign any contract, be sure to ask how many designs you will be shown for the agreed-upon price. Ask how many changes you can make without incurring additional costs. Be certain you know exactly what to expect.*

Why does this matter? Well, I suspect that you are spending money on your book to eventually sell it, tell a story, gain exposure for your work, hopefully attract attention with photography/art reviewers and perhaps gallery owners. They take their roles very seriously. They will pay close attention to the writing, and I promise you, the moment they pick up the book, they will open it to a page and within a half second, a mistake that was missed by your sister and lawyer husband will be glowing in neon pink. And that art reviewer will then pay extra close attention to each and every word, comma, and phrase in your book, all the while writing up a review that will appear for all to read. It's avoidable; don't go there.

The same is true for design and layout.

"My best friend's brother's cousin graduated from art school and works for a branding company. He can design it for half the cost of a real book designer, so I'll let him help me."

My question to them: "Has he ever designed a book?

Response: "Well, no."

My next question: "Does he have any idea how to construct a book in relation to its binding and what program(s) to build it in?"

And the response: "Well, I think he knows Photoshop, and he created a gorgeous logo for Pig Whistle BBQ!"

Not good enough. Entrust your book to people who know what they're doing. In the resources section, I list some editors, proofreaders, and designers for you to consider, but do your own research, too. Ask for names in your circle of friends and professionals. Meet with a few, review the books they've done, and then make your decision based on who you feel has the experience you need, a price you can afford, and the personality to be a comfortable and valuable part of your team.

As I mentioned earlier, many photographers have other creative talents beyond the camera. In some cases, photographers are also designers, although perhaps not book designers. If you fall into this category, can you design your own photography book? If you are willing to devote the time to studying how books are constructed, and learning a computer program needed to create them, then my answer would be "Yes."

*Many small, local publishers will use book editors and designers on a freelance basis. Call local publishers and ask who they use to edit, proofread and design their books. That is a wonderful way to find experienced professionals who know what they are doing.*

Teaching design is another book entirely. Teaching book design and layout is a sequel to that. And this is not either of those books. But I will offer some pointers to guide you in the direction you need to go. In addition to the pointers, if you read the sidebar to the right, I have also provided a link to some basic design templates that you can download and use to design your book. You can vary your design as you get comfortable with the process and become more familiar with the rules of good design.

Two of the most popular and readily acceptable software programs for book design are QuarkXpress and Adobe InDesign. Printers regularly receive book files in both. As a photographer, it's possible that you are already familiar with them. They are both wonderful programs for building books, with Adobe InDesign being my personal preference. I began designing books in PageMaker® in the late 1980s, and I find Adobe InDesign has an interface similar to both PageMaker and QuarkXpress. Chances are that, as a photographer, you have Adobe Creative Suite® versions 4, 5, or 6, and if it's the full version, then you already have Adobe InDesign as part of your package. That would be ideal because you wouldn't have to spend money on purchasing a new software program.

In regard to the design of your book, it would helpful for you to look at other photography books and how they are designed and laid out. Look closely at how many images per page are used, and the size of the margins. Do the images bleed off? Is each photograph treated the same on each page or does the layout have several ways of treating photographs? How many of the books have captions that appear with the photographs, and how many place captions at the back of the book?

Looking at these other books will help you see how different layouts create a mood and a feeling that works with the photography and guides the reader from page to page effortlessly. Ask yourself what the mood of your photography is and think about how to arrange the photographs to communicate that.

Examine the fonts that photography books use. Readability is important, and most often, simple is best. You don't want anything to compete with your photography; everything else should fall into the background and not be readily noticeable. If you use more than

## BOOK DESIGN TEMPLATES

*A great deal of thought and research goes into creating an effective book design. It's much more than just placing photographs on a page and dropping in text.*

*I carefully consider the subject matter, the intent of the author and what they want to communicate, the tone of the body of work, and I research the subject matter.*

*The information I gather influences my font choices, margin decisions, and placement of photographs and text. My goals are to create a book that doesn't look like any other book on the market and to create one that reflects the message the photographer wants to share with the reader.*

*Given that, I also understand that there may be those whose budget is limited and they cannot hire a book designer. For those individuals, I have designed a few very simple free design templates. I created them as InDesign files in a several different sizes and layouts. If you are familiar with InDesign, you can customize them to fit your size photograph and add or delete pages as needed.*

*You can download these from my website:www.howtopublishyour ownphotographybook.com.*

*Looking at other books will help you see how different layouts create a mood and feeling that works with the photography. Ask yourself what the mood of your photography is and think about how to arrange the photographs to communicate that.*

one font, try to stay with one font family, and don't use more than two different fonts in the book and on the cover jacket. I doubt you'll have many different types of text, so you really shouldn't have a need for more than that.

Suppose you have chosen to publish your book with a POD company. How do you design and produce a book with them? While the design principles remain the same, each POD company has its own methods to design a book. A few examples of POD companies include Viovio, MyPublisher, Shutterfly, and Blurb. I feel Blurb is producing some of the highest quality POD books, so let's examine their procedure to give you an idea of how it works.

Blurb has become quite popular because it allows many design options for your book as well as the ability to publish hardcover books with a jacket, or with what they call ImageWrap (similar to a printed litho case). This is where your art and book title are printed on paper that is then glued over the hard cover. Softcover is also available for a lower fee.

Blurb describes their books as bookstore-quality with library binding, but most of their books are perfect bound (glued), which is not library binding. Some of their books are side sewn, though side-sewn bindings won't open flat, which can be a problem for coffee-table books and portfolios. Blurb is constantly striving to increase the quality of their books, and their ProLine series is a result of that effort. Asukabook is the only company I've seen producing better quality POD books, but their prices are much higher and cost prohibitive in quantity.

When you visit the Blurb website, you will see that they offer seven book sizes, each with different price points, but with no custom sizes available. They give you a choice of paper stock with premium sheets costing more. For $7.95, you can order the Blurb Swatch Kit that has samples of their acid-free papers and samples of the linen cloth they use to cover hardcover books. You also have options for page count that allow you to create a book with as few as 20 pages and as high as 440—of course the price goes up with the page count. The ProLine series has a maximum page count of 240. Blurb offers four methods to begin creating your book:

- Blurb BookSmart®: This is their software program that you download and use to design your book. It seems to work well if you don't have a lot of pages, but for a book with page counts of fifty or more, it can slow the program down, and you will encounter problems.

- BLURB BOOKIFY™: Blurb supplies simple templates, already designed, that allow you to drop your photos into them and easily create a book. The site offers templates with themes such as graduation, wedding, cookbook, etc.

- PDF TO BOOK: This option allows you to use the computer program of your choice to design your book, then save it as a PDF file to their specific settings, and upload it for output. This option gives you more control over the design and layout of the book. You can use programs such as QuarkXpress, Microsoft Publisher®, whatever your preference, as long as you can convert it to a PDF for output. If you use Adobe InDesign, Blurb offers downloadable templates to help you with layout.

- HIRE AN EXPERT: Blurb gives you the option of using a designer whom you can hire to design your book for you. The designers are not Blurb employees. They are listed on the website through their BlurbNation Directory, along with links each designer's information. You can view their portfolios online and learn more about how they work before you choose one that fits your needs. This would be an additional cost, of course, but it's a nice option if you prefer not to design it yourself.

How much will a Blurb book cost? A 10" x 8" book using premium paper, 136 pages, no Blurb logo, with a dust jacket can cost $70. (It will cost a little less if you let Blurb put their logo on your book.) Blurb does offer volume discounts, however, if you want more than 125 copies, it may cost less using an offset printer—at least get quotes to compare. If you plan to sell only in their online bookstore, or if you only want ten to twenty-five copies, then POD is the way to go. For higher quality paper and cover cloth, Blurb's ProLine series is an option to consider, though the price will be higher.

Blurb promises to produce your book in five to six business days if you order less than twenty-five copies. Higher quantities take at least three additional days or even more if you have a truly high quantity. Standard shipping is five days unless you request expedited shipping. You won't know the final shipping cost until you upload your book.

## LIGHTROOM 4® BOOK MODULE

*Many photographers perform much of their photography processing and editing in Adobe Photoshop Lightroom. Version 4 was released with an innovative tool called the Book Module. It was developed in a collaborative effort between Blurb and Adobe to enable photographers to more easily create their own photography books in a streamlined process.*

*While Adobe InDesign is a powerful layout program that can be used to create your book, this Book Module option is a great alternative to creating your photography book without the learning curve needed to learn Adobe InDesign.*

*When you open Lightroom 4, you'll see "Book" on the top menu bar. You can use the auto layout feature to create a basic layout that you can adjust as needed, and you'll also find hundreds of predesigned layouts to choose from.*

*Once you are satisfied with how your book looks, you can easily soft-proof it and with the click of your mouse, connect to Blurb to quickly place an order for your printed and bound book.*

*For a tutorial with Adobe TV showing how to use Lightroom 4 Book Module, go to this URL: http://adobe.ly/yK56bp or scan this QR code.*

*Jose Antunes on the website photo tuts+ also has a great post on his personal experience using the Book Module. He even offers a free downloadable ebook that he created using Lightroom 4 Book Module. Go to this URL to read Jose's tutorial: http://bit.ly/J85tNm or scan this QR code.*

*The Book Module isn't just for printed books, you can also use it to create an ebook or a PDF portfolio of your work, something that previously was best done by using a graphics layout program like Adobe InDesign. On The Lightroom Lab website, David Marx writes in detail, along with a video, about how to create a professional looking ebook and/or PDF portfolio of your photography. To see it, go to this URL: http://bit.ly/zjRaE2 or scan this QR code.*

*Take advantage of Lightroom's auto-update option so that you can keep your version of software current with its newest features.*

*Last, I recommend that you join Blurb's email list. They are constantly sending out discounts and special deals for their services that you won't want to miss out on!*

Whatever POD company you choose, research other people's experiences to help you choose a company. On pages 106 and 107 of this book, I have included a POD-at-a-Glance chart that compares the differences between four popular POD companies, including Blurb. Keep in mind that this is just a snapshot in time. These POD companies change their pricing and offerings often. For updated information, go to this book's website, and go to the resources section to view the latest chart comparisons: www.HowtoPublishYourOwnPhotographyBook.com.

One problem I've read about and experienced with POD companies, is that they use many different facilities to print books, resulting in inconsistent quality, color, binding, and materials. If ordered at different times, one of your books may come from Washington, another from Alabama, another from New Jersey, and they can all look very different in color and construction. Jason Dunn, executive editor of the website www.DigitalHomeThoughts.com, wrote an in-depth article on POD. It's called "The Great Photo Round-up Review: Who Makes the Best Photo Books?" He published a photo documentary book of his wife's pregnancy and their first child. He worked with twelve POD companies and reports on the experience, the customer service, and final book quality of each. It's a very interesting read: www.digitalhomethoughts.com/news/show/97676/. But, as I've mentioned before, Blurb is still my current favorite of all the POD companies.

Now let's look at the structure of a sewn, hard-cover photography book. It has four main components.

1. Cover: a hard case covered in material (book jacket is optional), or softcover. Glued to the book boards are endpapers that hold the book block in the cover case.

2. Interior front matter which includes:
   · half title page (if your book has a subtitle, you omit it on this page)

Book Block

Front-folded endpaper glued to cover board

Back-folded endpaper glued to cover board

Boards covered in cloth or paper

Smyth-sewn signature sections and glued spine

- Full-title spread (a spread means two pages facing each other)
- Copyright or colophon page (can also be placed in the back matter)
- Dedication
- Table of contents
- Essay, foreword, preface, and/or an introduction

3. Body of the book showing your photographs
4. Back matter of the book, which includes:
   - Artist/photographer afterword, if one does not appear in the front matter
   - Captions (if the information does not appear in the body of the book)
   - Photographer biography
   - Acknowledgments
   - Copyright or colophon (if it does not appear in the front matter)

Will you number your pages? Numbering makes it easier for a reader to navigate back through the book if they want to search for something specific. Pages of a book typically show page numbers (folios) printing on the first page following the table of contents, even though the numeration actually begins on the first page of the book.

Look at the beginning of this book. The page numbers don't print on the page until after the table of contents, but the very next page shows the number *vi*. That is a lowercase Roman numeral and those should be used in the front matter of the book, changing to Arabic numerals when the body of the book begins (1, 2, 3). Now move forward to page 1 titled The Plan. That's where the body of the book begins and an Arabic numeral is used to mark that first page of the body; therefore we begin again using the actual number 1. Now the book continues to print the page numbers sequentially through to the last page unless a photograph or graphic prevents it. And remember: odd numbers are always on the right, and even numbers always appear on the left. Look at other books and and how they treat page numbering. You'll find some that deviate from this, but I am offering you the traditional publishing standard.

The copyright or colophon page, as I introduced above, will normally appear on page iv of conventionally published books. But, with art and photography books, many times you want

BIND YOUR OWN BOOKS

*Perhaps you want a few copies of your book, and you'd prefer not to create them POD, but you still want a beautiful book showcasing your photography. Another option is to print and bind your own books by hand. I've made both soft- and hard-cover books—as many as fifty copies of the same book.*

*While a bit time consuming because it's detailed work, it's not really difficult and the result can be very rewarding. Creating your own hand-bound books is truly an art in itself. Go to your bookstore, or search online and you will find many books that demonstrate various methods for constructing, gluing, sewing, and binding your book. There are also blogs, websites, DVDs, and YouTube videos with step-by-step instructions for making every type of binding you can imagine.*

*In many cities you can even find workshops that will teach you the art of hand-bound books. Check out your local art centers, galleries, colleges, and even art supply stores—many will offer classes with local artists. In Philadelphia, you can visit the Philadelphia Center for the Book. Founded in 2005, it celebrates the book as a contemporary art form bringing artists, educators, and the public together for readings, ex-hibits and workshops. You can also visit my website where I have posted some common handbound book bind-ing methods.*

*Your handbound book is a limited edition piece of art, and you might want to consider numbering each copy. A numbered edition is where the total number of copies in the print run is notated on the book: 1 of 50, 2 of 50, and so on.*

*Bottom line: don't be afraid to experi-ment with binding your own book.*

to move your reader more quickly into the body of the book so that they aren't slowed down by too much front matter. It is acceptable to place the copyright information in the back mat-ter. This is the page that will have details on how the book was published, including copyright, credits, and contact information.

As you review other photography books, you will notice that many will have an intro-duction written by an art critic, curator, well-known photographer, or an expert related to the subject matter of the photographs appearing in the book. This is an important thing to consider for your book. Does your photography relate to public health? Is it focused on the environ-ment? Does it document a cultural issue that is current in society? Think about your theme and who might be a good person to write an introduction for your book. The more well-known the person, the better, because it can help gain exposure for your work. Create a short list of peo-ple who might be a good match for your book. Do not be intimidated by your chosen candidate's level of fame; be assertive and respectful when you approach him or her. Make it easy for them to visualize the final published book. You'll want to send them prints of your work, an artist essay, and if you can, create a color mock-up of the book from your own printer or have one printed at a local graphics services company. Adhere the pages back-to-back and cleanly tape the binding. You can also use two-sided paper, which will save you all the work of taping the pages. Make this as easy as possible for the person you are contacting to visualize how the book will look.

You will have people turn you down; everyone is busy and overwhelmed with their own responsibilities. So if this happens, do not take it personally. Simply move on to the next per-son on your list. Other times, your request will be granted, but you will be asked to pay a fee. However I've found that if you ask people whose industry or cause might also benefit from being connected to your work, they are more than happy to write your introduction. Offer a photographic print in addition to some copies of the final book as a thank-you to your writer for having taken considerable time to write the introduction. Give him or her plenty of lead time to do this for you; do not ask for the introduction in a rush or you risk losing the writer.

And remember, however you create your book, have an experienced proofreader proof each page and the book jacket before you send your final files to the printer!

Okay, fasten your seatbelts and hold onto your hat. This section, a plethora of information, contains important details you need to know—do not be afraid!

Considering the time, talent, energy, and money that you've invested in publishing your book, you may be concerned about how to protect your copyright. First there is the issue of your photographs, and second, is the issue of your book.

When you take a photograph, you have created something entirely new, a unique representation of what you see and how you see it. Copyright law states that the moment you put it in a tangible form that can be viewed by another person, it is automatically copyright protected. That tangible form can be a print, slide, transparency, a website, or a digital file that exists on a disk, At that point, you have secured copyright, and current U.S. copyright law states that you own exclusive rights for the duration of your lifetime plus seventy years. To show evidence of your copyright, you should place a copyright symbol, ©, next to your name, and it should appear wherever your photograph appears in print or online, for example "© Your Name." You can also add a date if you like, such as "©2010 Your Name." In a digital file, you should also encode your copyright symbol, name, and date in the meta data, which is located in "file info," which can be found beneath "Info" on the menu bar in Adobe Photoshop®.

Above and beyond these methods of protection, there are additional practices that can help you if, in fact, you need to prove ownership in a court of law due to infringement. However, following these procedures is not required to secure copyright, and therefore, some photographers do not do it because it can be time consuming if you take a lot of photographs.

- You can encode a watermark into your digital image.
- You can add the words "All Rights Reserved" beside your copyright symbol, and this is honored within the courts of the United States but not necessarily everywhere else in the world. You can take the additional step of registering in other countries, which might be worth considering if you do travel photography or documentary photography that takes you abroad.

*Locating the copyright symbol © on your keyboard depends on the computer you are using.*

*For a PC, there are two methods:*
*1. Hold down Alt and type 0169 on the number pad (right-hand side of your keyboard).*
*2. Go to "insert," check "symbols," and click on the copyright symbol.*

*On a Macintosh computer:*
*Hold down the option key at the same time you press G. You can also go under "insert," select "symbol" and then "advanced symbol" and then click on the copyright symbol.*

- You can "publish" your photography, which means to exhibit and sell, to lease or loan, or to transfer ownership. At that point, your work is "published," and you are subject to mandatory deposit, which means you should send two copies to the Library of Congress within five years of publication in order to establish "prima facie," which is Latin meaning "at first appearance." If registered within three months of publication and before a copyright infringement, then you are entitled to statutory damages and attorney fees in a lawsuit. This is very important if you want monetary compensation for work that is infringed. You can also register images in bulk. Here is the address of where to send those two copies of your work with a letter stating that you are complying with mandatory deposit:

  > Library of Congress
  > Copyright Office-CAD 407
  > 101 Independence Avenue, SE
  > Washington, DC  20559-6607

- You can also register your photographs with the U.S. Copyright Office, which will create a legal, public record of ownership. The same timelines apply here as in mandatory deposit. Registration may be made at any time during the life of the photograph to create the public record. Copyright registration can be made by going to this website: www.copyright.gov. There are three methods for registering your work:

  1. You can file online for a $35 filing fee.
  2. You can download form CO, which includes a barcode for easy processing. You fill out the form and mail it in with a $50 filing fee.
  3. You can download form VA, which has no barcode. Fill out the form and mail it in with a $65 filing fee.

So what about your book and protecting ownership of that? Your book will contain your photographs as well as the text that you have written, housed in a nicely designed package with a book title. To display ownership, you will need to include copyright information on the copyright or colophon page of your book. If you are self-publishing, you will want to include all necessary information and your copyright page should look something like this:

Published by
Your name or company name
1234 Street Address
City, State  Zip

© 2010 Your Name. All rights reserved.
No part of this book may be reproduced in any form or by any means without the prior written permission of the Publisher, excepting brief quotations used in conjunction with reviews that are written specifically for use in a professional newspaper, magazine, or online publication.

First Edition
Printed in (country where book is manufactured)
Library of Congress #:  2010933590
ISBN #:  978-0-2260234-2-1

Before you publish your book, you should get a Preassigned Control Number (PCN) from the Library of Congress. This number identifies your book and is recorded in a catalog at the Library of Congress, and the book is then part of the national library  databases. This is free, and you can easily register for one at this website: http://www.loc.gov/publish/pcn/. It will tell you all about the program and how to apply and receive your number. You will fill out an online request to participate in the program. When you are accepted, you will receive a password to use to log into the PCN program, fill out a submission form, and request a number for your book. The number will come to you electronically, and you will print that number on your copyright page (see example on previous page.) Once you receive your book from the printer, you will send a copy to the Library of Congress for their archives. On the next page is the address to send your book to. Be sure to include a letter that states you are complying with the requirements of the PCN program.

Library of Congress
US & Publisher Liaison Division
Cataloging in Publication Program
101 Independence Avenue, S.E.
Washington, DC  20540-4283

Maybe you're really on a roll, and you've just published your tenth book of photography! For your eleventh, you can switch from the PCN system of cataloging to the Cataloging in Publication (CIP) Program at the Library of Congress. You can learn more details by scanning the QR code on the right or going to their website: http://www.loc.gov/publish/cip/.

*Learn about the CIP program with the Library of Congress by scanning the QR code above or by navigating to this URL: www.loc.gov/publish/cip.*

One question you might have is: "What can I NOT copyright?" You cannot copyright the book concept, design, layout, color scheme, or the title of your book. Even so, it might be wise for you to search book titles just to make sure you aren't duplicating the title of a book currently published that could be confused with yours.

Finally let's talk about ISBNs, which, if you are self-publishing you will purchase through Bowker, a company we first talked about on page 11 and for which we created a budget entry to purchase the ISBN on page 11.

Bowker, founded in 1872, collects extensive book title and publisher information in the United States and other countries, which has made it the world's leading source of bibliographic information for the publishing industry. It offers many services to publishers and is the official U.S. agency where you will purchase an ISBN for your book. The ISBN is a 13-digit number that identifies the publisher of a book, its country of origin, the original language in which the book was printed, and the book title. This information makes the book searchable by databases all over the world and is a necessity in order to sell your book online, in gift shops, and in bookstores.

You have the option of purchasing a single ISBN for $125, or you can buy them in larger blocks, which save money if you publish more than one book. First, you will apply for an application to be accepted into the ISBN account system. You will be given a pass-

*You can order an ISBN by scanning the QR code above or by navigating to this URL: https://www.myidentifiers. com/index.php?ci_id=1479*

*An example of an Bookland EAN Barcode with its five-digit add-on.*

*You can order a Bookland EAN Barcode by scanning the QR code below and by navigating to this URL: https://commerce.bowker.c om/BarCode/default.asp*

word and access to manage your account online. Then you will fill out the necessary information, and your ISBN(s) will be sent to you electronically via email. Print that ISBN on the copyright page of your book. Scan the QR code at top left or go to this URL to order your ISBNs online: https://www.myidentifiers.com/index.php?ci_id=1479.

You will also need a barcode for the book jacket. This allows the bookstore or retailer to scan your barcode and process sales transactions. Books have a special barcode called a Bookland EAN Barcode. You can order this from the Bowker website as well, once you have your ISBN number, which will be encoded into the barcode itself. You can also encode the list price of your book, which is required by most vendors. Barcodes are $25 each, but if you are publishing more than one book at a time, you can get quantity discounts. Scan the QR code at bottom left when you are ready to order a barcode.

Retailers require the Bookland EAN Barcode, so take care not to to order a regular barcode. Regular barcodes don't have the extension numbers and bars on the right like the barcode shown at left. It has a 13-digit code that starts with the Bookland prefix 978 or 979. After that are the first nine digits of your ISBN number, followed by a check digit. The small five-digit add-on begins with a number representing the country code: 6 for Canada and 5 for the United States. The last four digits are the price of the book. U.S. books priced $99 or more print 59999.

Once your book is published, you will need to log on to your Bowker account and register your title with their Books In Print® program. This officially registers your ISBN with Bowker and makes it active in the system, enabling people to search for and order your book.

All of this may seem daunting, but once you absorb the information, you'll see that this entire section boils down to three things you need to address for your book:

1. Copyright
2. Library of Congress PCN acquisition
3. ISBN and Bookland EAN Barcode from Bowker

It doesn't take too much time, and it allows people to find, order, and purchase your book, which is a great thing!

You've taken your photographs, processed them to look the best they can, and designed a book around them. So your job is about over now, right? Not by a long shot.

As you look out into the world, your eyes have the ability to see millions of shades of color and tone. With your camera, you take photographs that capture a single moment in time allowing that moment to stand still. Your images are your interpretation of that experience; they document what you saw and how it felt when you watched that zebra race past you as it was being chased by police cars during the afternoon rush hour. (True story!) Honestly, who would believe you if you didn't have the photographic evidence to prove it? With photography, you can stop that moment and transfer it into a form that allows you to share the experience and emotion with others, but they will never be able to see exactly what you saw. Your job is to get them as close as possible.

When you process your photographs in a darkroom or digitally, you take excruciating care that the highlights, midtones, and shadows are perfectly balanced. Unfortunately a photographic print cannot record all of the colors and tones that your eye was able to see. Quality control begins here and will continue all the way through the printing of the pages of your book. As your photograph is recorded in other forms, it has a limited ability to reproduce all the colors that you were able to see with your own eyes. And as you proceed through the printing of your book, as shown in the chart below, the ability to reproduce those colors and tones drops exponentially.

| NUMBER OF COLOR SHADES | MEASURED PERCEPTION AND REPRODUCTION | PERCENTAGE |
|---|---|---|
| 16,777,216 | Computer Monitor, 24 bit | 100% |
| 7,000,000 | Human Eye | 42% |
| 2,500,000 | Photographic Reproduction (continuous tone) | 12% |
| 2,500,000 | Dye-Sublimation Printer (continuous tone) | 12% |
| 65,000 | Digital Inkjet Color Proof (dithering technology) *provided by a printing company prior to going on press* | .004% |
| 2,000 | 4/Color Process Sheetfed Offset Printing (halftone) | .0001% |

You might be asking yourself: "The numbers in that chart are interesting, but how is this information relevant to me?"

It's relevant because as you begin looking at prepress digital proofs and perhaps even press check proofs, you need to:

1. Keep in mind that your images will not look exactly the same as your photographic print.

2. Examine the proofs closely and ask questions you might have such as: "Is it possible to achieve a deeper black here?" or "There is too much red in this person's face. Is there a way to pull some of that out?" You can even talk in percentages if you feel comfortable: "Please bring down the cyan in this image by 10 percent."

While you are asking questions and giving direction, you need to think about that chart and be realistic about what's possible. Remember: you will never be able to reproduce exactly what you see, so quality control is essential to making your photo look as good as possible!

Another good question to ask is: "Before I send my book to the printer, what can I do to improve color management?" You can do several things.

1. Calibrate your computer monitor as well as your printer if you are working with digital versions of your photographs. I don't mean the standard calibration instructions that accompany each computer. I mean purchasing and installing professional software that syncs with your printer so that what you see there is what outputs on your printer and creates a profile that you can share with others. I use Spyder 4, and it's worked well for my needs, and I've also heard good things about Huey Pro. I hesitate even recommending these since technology changes so fast and more-improved resources are developed every day. In the 1990s, I bought a brand new Quadra 700 computer that I had researched, read great reviews on, and was very excited about. The very next day, an article in a prominent computer magazine stated, "The Quadra is a dead end Mac. Don't buy it!" I was crushed. The point is, there are many different programs at various price points, so do your research, read the reviews, and choose one that works best for your needs and fits

*Remember: you will never be able to reproduce exactly what you see, so quality control is essential to making your photo look as good as possible!*

within your budget. The best time to buy is when you need it! (And that Quadra? It turned out to be a great workhorse and just what I needed!)

2. Create prints of your photographs that you are happy with and are closest to how you want them to appear in your book. These, in conjunction with your files, can help your printer see what you're going for.

3. Find a printer with strict-quality color management procedures such as Four Colour Print Group or consider hiring a company like the one I mentioned earlier in the book, iocolor. They've developed an extremely effective way to manage color printing on an offset printing press. Iocolor will take your book file, with all of your high-resolution images, create a custom ICC color profile for you, and link it to the printing press you plan to print on, anywhere in the world. They contact your printer directly, set the calibration, and then generate high-quality color proofs that are then used as proofs to match on press. And they will communicate directly with the printer if problems arise on press. It's very precise and effective.

Why is all this so necessary? Once you process your photograph to look a certain way, why is it so difficult to maintain that through the printing process? Isn't it all the same type of information? Is it simply due to how many color shades can be reproduced? Well, no, there are other aspects that come into play. One of these is color space, and the other is halftone.

Let's start with color space. Your computer monitor emits color as light. As you may remember from your science class (if you weren't dozing at your desk), all the colors of the spectrum together create white light. Do you recall that prism experiment in which a beam of white light passing through a prism separated the color spectrum? All of those colors are composed of three primary colors: red, green, and blue (RGB). When you subtract from these colors in different ways, it creates secondary colors and all the other colors you can see on your computer. When you view your photograph on a computer screen, you are viewing it as light and variations of those three color components.

Images on paper, canvas, or board are composed of pigments such as toner, paint, or ink, not light. The three primary colors for pigment are magenta, cyan, and yellow—light reflects off of them allowing you to see the color. You create other colors and tones by mixing and adding them together, which is the opposite of what your computer monitor does. Creating other colors with light is a subtractive process, while creating colors on paper is an additive process. Still with me?

Without delving into too much color theory, you can see how that alone can impact the difference in how something looks on a computer and how it looks on a reflective piece of paper. The term *color space* refers to the spectrum of colors (the range or the gamut) that is possible within a specific format. RBG on your monitor has one range of possible colors; and reflective magenta, cyan, and yellow have a different, yet overlapping, range of possible colors. Let's complicate things a little bit more and introduce CMYK, which stands for "cyan, magenta, yellow, and black." But wait—the fourth letter of that acronym is *K*, and it stands for "black"? Yes. In the financial world, a K stands for $1,000, in CMYK color space, it represents black.

CMYK is a combination of inks used in the traditional printing of magazines, newspapers, brochures, and books. By traditional printing, I am referring to offset lithography. The density of these four inks cannot be varied, so in order to reproduce a vast spectrum of colors on paper, they are halftoned. This is where each translucent ink is converted into a varying degree of dots and placed at a distinct angle. Then the grid of dots for each ink are printed overlapping each other in order to build the photograph or image on paper. In lighter areas, the dots will be smaller in size, and, in darker areas, they will be larger. If you look at a book with a magnifying glass, you can see the dot pattern.

When you prepare your photograph for printing on an offset printing press, you must convert that image from its RGB format to a CMYK format, which means you will be moving from one color space to another. This will affect the colors and shades in your image. In addition, you make this conversion on a computer where your monitor is based in RGB. When you make that conversion, the monitor emits a simulation of what the image will look like in CMYK; it's not an exact representation. What you get on press will look a little different from what your computer screen is showing you.

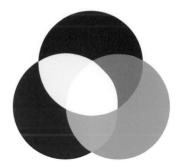

*This shows the subtractive color process in light emitted from your computer monitor beginning with the three primary colors of the light spectrum: red, green, and blue.*

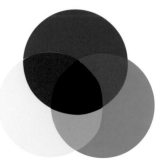

*This shows the additive color process in reflected light from pigment on a piece of paper beginning with the three primary colors: magenta, cyan, and yellow.*

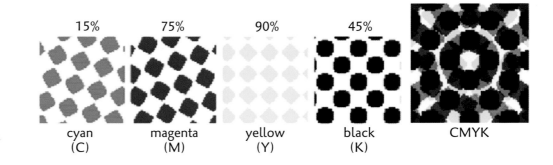

| 15% | 75% | 90% | 45% | |
| --- | --- | --- | --- | --- |
| cyan (C) | magenta (M) | yellow (Y) | black (K) | CMYK |

*As you can see in the example on the right, the CMYK inks are printed at different angles. If they were printed at the same angle, the result would be a distracting moiré pattern of dots in the image.*

In very high-end print reproduction, there is another type of halftone called stochastic screening also known as FM screening, which stands for "frequency modulation." This system still uses dots, but they are much smaller than those used in traditional halftoning. They also differ in that the dots remain the same size. In this system, the dots are positioned in something like a dithering pattern that mimics continuous tone. Four Colour Print Group has its own variation of this called Sublima, which is a hybrid process whereby both stochastic and traditional halftoning are used to print the images.

"What about POD?" you ask. "Isn't POD digital printing? Wouldn't I be working in the same color space and thus get a better print?" And "Looking back at the color shade chart on page 51, it shows digital printing as reproducing 65,000 colors as opposed to 2,000 with offset printing, so that means I'll get more colors printing POD digitally, right?" These are all good questions. And here are the answers.

Since we've previously used Blurb as an example of a POD company, I'll continue to discuss their methods. (Remember that there are many POD companies to investigate and their procedures can be quite different.) Blurb does print their books digitally, as do all POD companies. For the interiors of their books, they use the HP Indigo Digital-Offset Press. (Covers may be printed on other inkjet printers depending on the facility where your book is manufactured.) This is a high-speed printer that can print a short run of pages very quickly. However, if you take a magnifying glass and look closely at a book printed with Blurb, you will see that it has a traditional halftone dot pattern. That's because it doesn't print with the continuous tone of a dye sublimation printer or with the dithering technology of a standard inkjet; it simulates offset lithography with dots. The quality still does not match that of traditional offset. Will that improve over time? I suspect it will, but for now, offset is superior.

What about other POD companies? LuLu also uses the CMYK color space with dot patterns simulating offset and, like Blurb, delivers a product that does not exactly match offset printing. If you use a POD company, your key to getting the best quality book you can is to find out what kind of printer the company is using, what its color space is, and then ask them what you can expect to happen during printing in regard to brightness, contrast, etc. Ask if there are specific steps you can take to prepare your images for their particular output. If the company's books tend to print dark, you can lighten your photographs to accommodate that expected result. If they use the CMYK color space, would they prefer to do the conversion of your photographs from RGB on their end, so that they can adjust it to their equipment more accurately than you could do? Blurb's HP printer automatically makes that conversion for you before printing your book, although Blurb does allow you to you make your own conversion and even offers tips as to how to do that and what ICC color profile to use. Managing color with POD books can be difficult and sometimes even frustrating, so the more you know and prepare for, the better your photographs, and your book, will look.

What about proofs before your book is finally printed? What can you expect from a conventional publisher, your printer, your POD company? Your publisher will provide you with color proofs to view before going to press. This is your last chance before printing begins to note any glaring mistakes in the text, as well as to make comments on color, yet keeping in mind that what you are viewing are inkjet color prints. Final tweaking of color can be done on press while the pages are being printed, and the publisher always has someone doing a "press check" for quality control to manage that process.

If you are self-publishing, the printer will send you inkjet color proofs as well as blue-line proofs (in England they are called ozalids). These are not provided for color, rather they show the text, images, and page sequencing of your book. Proof the text one final time as well as confirming the correct order of the pages. You do have the option of being on press with the book if you so choose. The pressmen and women use the digital color proofs as a guide to

## USING COLOR PROFILES

*So you are self-publishing and you've received an ICC color profile from your printer. What do you do with it?*

*The first thing you need to do is copy it into the correct folder in your hard drive so that it's accessible.*

*On a Mac platform, copy the .icc file into the MacHD ›› Library ›› Color Sync ›› Profile folder.*

*For PC Adobe users, you must rename .icc file extensions to .icm. Once you've done that, right-click the file and it will automatically install for you.*

*You are now prepared to convert your files from RGB to CMYK. If you are not comfortable making the conversion, your printer's prepress department can do it for you, though it may involve an additional charge. To make the conversion yourself, open your images in Adobe Photoshop. Go to EDIT ›› ConvertToProfile ›› select the file you installed. Then save the image in CMYK. If you see significant color changes occur, you can continue to tweak the color, though it may not be possible to make it appear exactly as it did in RGB mode. When all of your images have been converted, you will need to relink or update them in your page layout program.*

*This is not a technical manual, so for more detailed color management information, scan the QR code at the top of the next page.*

*A QR code that links to very detailed information on color theory, color management, and ICC color profiles. Written by San Diego photographer, Gary G. Ballard, it's very thorough information, though not for the faint of heart. www.gballard.net/psd/cms theory.html*

*A QR code that links to Blurb's color management tips when using BookSmart. http://www.blurb.com/guides/color_management/image_prep_booksmart*

*A QR code that links to Blurb's color management tips for their PDF to book process. http://www.blurb.com/guides/color_management/image_prep_pdf*

check color as sheets come off the press. A press sheet is taken to a 5,000 kelvin light-filled booth, and it's set alongside the color digital proof. This is where you can say, "I see a blue cast that isn't in the inkjet proof. Is there anything we can do on press to eliminate that?" or "There isn't enough black in those shadows. Is it possible to darken those?" Be respectful and ask the pressmen their expert opinion. They are craftsmen, they know their machines, and they know color. They want to make your book the best it can be. If you are in another country on press, you may need to ask for help with translation if your pressmen don't speak much English.

If your book is printing in China, and you aren't able to make the trip to Hong Kong, don't feel as if you at the mercy of the pressmen. One thing you can do is ask how much it would cost for a "wet proof." This is an actual press proof where they run a few pages on an actual press and send them to you for approval. If this is your dilemma, ask if your printer can provide wet proofs and what the fee would be. I have done this, and it has made the process so much smoother and certainly eased my mind. Once the pages are printed, the printer will send you F&Gs, which stands for "folded and gathered sheets." These are your printed book pages folded down and trimmed. This is your last chance to make changes if you should find a glaring error. While it will cost money to reprint, you can still make a change before binding.

And what about POD? Blurb recommends you do a "soft proof" of your book using their ICC color profile. This is a link to the procedure if you use their program BookSmart: http://www.blurb.com/guides/color_management/image_prep_booksmart. This is for PDF to book: http://www.blurb.com/guides/color_management/image_prep_pdf. Adobe Lightroom 4 Book Module offers a streamlined system to soft proof your book with Blurb. Investigate what the procedure is for other POD companies; it's worth the effort.

There are facts that exist for photography, offset printing, color space, and POD, and then there are varying opinions, approaches, and techniques in working with and applying these facts. Many people have different truths about how to negotiate within these parameters. I can't know or share with you all of them, but what I can do is tell you the facts and share my experience to help you publish the best photography book possible within your specific parameters. Then I hope you'll share your experience with me.

DEFINITION OF MARKETING:
The difference between selling your book and having a
six-foot wall of books in your guest bedroom upstairs.

If you've been fortunate enough to land a publisher, then they will develop a marketing plan specific to your book and its market. The plan will include distribution, media kits, sales materials, preparing for review requests, website development, scheduling media interviews, twitter communication, and blog creation, without giving you the responsibility for creating or funding it. But keep in mind: publishers have had to significantly scale back their budgets for promoting books. While they will do some limited marketing, it will be up to you to play a very active role in helping to implement their plan and supplement it in every way you can with your own resources.

If you are self-publishing, this is the stage where most first-time authors really drop the ball because they don't know how to market. Your book is becoming a reality, but now what? People won't buy a book that they don't even know exists, so a marketing plan is crucial.

Take a deep breath, go get a cup of coffee, and then let's get started—there's a lot of work ahead. We'll start with a question: At what point in the process of publishing your book should you begin developing your marketing plan? Answer: From day one.

When you began your book, you definitely had a reason for believing that there is a percentage of the public who will want or need your book. Hopefully you've been taking notes and creating a profile for that particular target market and its purchasing behaviors.

Who are they, and how can you reach them?

Where do they go to learn and read about photography?

Where do they go to view and purchase photography?

Where do they go to buy a book like the one you are publishing?

If you haven't already, finalize the process of identifying in detail who your target

*People won't buy a book that they don't even know exists, so a marketing plan is crucial to the success of your book.*

market is and the various ways you can reach these readers so that you can develop your marketing plan before your book is sent to the printer.

"What's the rush?" you ask. "Won't I have plenty of time for that while the books are being printed and bound?" Actually, no. You want to approach your marketing in the same way a publishing company does—with plenty of lead time to create a buzz about your book before it even gets printed. In addition, things happen on an industry-driven schedule when you are preparing to launch your book to the public. If you fail to follow what the industry expects, you may fail to secure distribution, reviews for your book, and valuable sales. Do you even need or want a distributor for a photography book? That's a really good question, and we'll look at that in a few moments.

To begin, we'll examine a schedule first and then move on to the details of what your marketing plan should include. This is a lot of information, and it may seem overwhelming at first. Realistically, not every author can accomplish each task I list here. But I feel it is my responsibility and in your best interest to demonstrate what a best-practice marketing plan involves, and then it is up to you to customize it for what your can truly accomplish.

Below is a timeline to guide you through the creation of a standard book-publishing marketing and publicity plan:

1.  Identify your target market the moment you begin working on your book. Photography is a niche market, so be very clear about where your potential sales will come from.

2.  Immediately make a detailed list of bookstores, retail stores, galleries, organizations, photography clubs and associations, photography supply stores, online bookstores, etc., where you can reach your target audience.

3.  If you don't already have one, begin creating an email database of names that you can send email-blasts to and announce your book and book signings.

4.  Begin compiling a list of places you can send your book for reviews. A conventionally published book is typically sent to: *The New York Times Book Review*, Kirkus, *The Los Angeles Book Review*, *The Midwest Book Review*, *National Geographic Book Review*,

*Publisher's Weekly, School and Library* Journal etc. But do your own research for your niche market and the theme of your photography, and then build your list of names and addresses of fifty or seventy-five places where, if you got a good review, it could help you sell a lot of books. Don't forget photography magazines, online and print!

5   Five months before the printing and binding of your book is completed, write your marketing plan with a budget attached to secure a distributor and publicist. I'll list the details of that later in this section of the book.

6.  Four to five months before the printing and binding of your book is completed, begin approaching distributors for your book. What is a distributor? A book distributor has established relationships with booksellers and retail stores. They do four important things:

   - warehouse your book and make it available for sale
   - include your book title and description in sales materials and catalogs presented to booksellers who are looking to purchase
   - process orders and distribute your book to stores
   - handle and process returns from bookstores (yes, bookstores can return unsold books)

For many years, it was impossible to get a major distributor to even work with a self-published author. While still a challenge, it is now possible to find a distributor who will work with you as long as the book is of high-quality construction and you have a marketing and promotions plan in place.

Now let's go back to that question on the previous page: Do you really need a national book distributor? Most likely, large bookstore chains are not where you will sell most of your photography books, and that is where distributors will make your book available. The majority of your sales will probably come from photography clubs, photography supply stores, exhibit openings, galleries, your website, online photography bookstores, local independent bookstores (that you don't need a distributor to get into), and wherever else you can reach your market, So you will need to decide if national distribution is something you want to include, or if you can be creative and aggressive in how to target potential buyers of your book.

One thing you should know if you are printing your book POD: you won't be able to secure a distributor because they require a large quantity of books to warrant their efforts in making it available for sale on a national level. Quality is also an issue; they demand that books be the same quality as they receive from publishing companies.

7. Unless you have a publicist working with you, you will need to write a press release and create a professional looking press kit (also called a media kit) in both hard copy and digital form that can be used online and also saved to a CD or DVD. What should be in that press kit? I'll describe it in further detail in the Publicity section.

8. If you are going for national distribution, then do not exclude this step of the process. Four months before the printing and binding of your book is complete, print about fifty prepublication review copies of your book. These are also called "Uncorrected Proofs," and those two words should be printed on the cover in type that is easy to read. You can print these copies digitally and have them perfect bound in softcover with all of your distribution, publicity, and sales information on the back cover. Even if you don't go for national distribution, have a smaller number of prepublication review copies printed—you still need to send them out for reviews to use in your marketing plan. Here is an example of how the information should read:

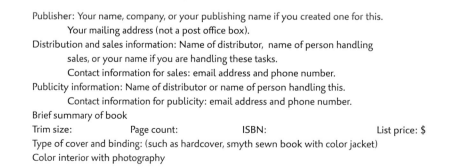

Publisher: Your name, company, or your publishing name if you created one for this.
　　Your mailing address (not a post office box).
Distribution and sales information: Name of distributor, name of person handling
　　sales, or your name if you are handling these tasks.
　　Contact information for sales: email address and phone number.
Publicity information: Name of distributor or name of person handling this.
　　Contact information for publicity: email address and phone number.
Brief summary of book
Trim size:　　　　　　Page count:　　　　ISBN:　　　　　　　　List price: $
Type of cover and binding: (such as hardcover, smyth sewn book with color jacket)
Color interior with photography

## Prepublication/Advance Review Copies

*If you just don't have the funds to print twenty-five or fifty prepublication review copies at a local printer or POD, then consider printing only ten and send them to the reviewers you are most likely to get a response from.*

*If you can't afford even that, then print out several copies of your book on double-sided paper with trim marks. Trim the pages yourself, or ask your local quick printer if they have a cutting machine to trim them for you (and if so, be sure to ask how much it would cost).*

*Next, print out covers of your book with bleed (bleed is when the color of your cover extends $1/8$" beyond the trim size) and DON'T trim it down. Then ask your printer what they would charge to glue the covers to your trimmed pages and then trim the cover down flush with the body of the book. If you can afford to have them do this, it will probably be a lot less expensive than using POD. The worst case scenario is you glue the cover to the pages yourself and create your own perfect bound book. Look online for how-to instructions and YouTube videos.*

Depending on the trim size and page count, you can digitally print and bind the books at one of your local printers for around $1,000. Yes, that number has three zeros in it. If you aren't going for national distribution and decide to print only twenty-five copies, then perhaps your investment will be more like $750. Shop around for cheaper quotes. Some publishing companies use POD services to print their prepublication review copies although a photography book with a lot of pages could get expensive using POD. Get cost estimates on soft cover and decide which is most economical for you. This is indeed costly but necessary if you have landed a distributor. Why? Because an important and expected publishing practice is sending out prepublication review copies to book reviewers all over the country. However, they won't review a published book; they will only review uncorrected proofs three to four months prior to publication of the book. They require a lot of advance notice to read the book, write a review, and then print that review in their publications. I'll talk about this in more detail later in the Publicity section of this book.

Remember that list you made in step number four on pages 60–61? Those are the places you should send your prepublication review copies. Find out what their submission requirements are (if they post any) and follow those instructions to the letter. Thank them in advance for their generous consideration. Send out the copies and hope for one or two good reviews. Don't be offended: it's not that I think you'll get bad reviews, it's simply that self-published books are a bit harder to get reviews for and reviewers are swamped with requests. They have a limited amount of time and only review a small percentage of what they receive. If you are working with a publicist, you can give him or her the copies to send out for review. It might be a good idea to ask them for a list of who they are contacting, and you can send out some to your own list.

The rest of the prepublication review copies you can give to peers, art critics, professional photographers, photography curators, etc., and request reviews from them. Hold a few back to send to your short list of people you want to request an introduction from, and then hold one or two back for your own needs. Make a file as you get responses and keep a copy of each review. Plan to print a couple of the best reviews directly on your book jacket. You can use them in your marketing and publicity materials as well. Good reviews sell books. Do everything in your power to get them.

If you simply do not have the financial resources to produce any prepublication review copies, then perhaps you can get a few reviews by sending color copies off your printer and approaching a well-known person in photography or an art critic who would write a review that you can use in marketing. Be sure to package the book very professionally and thank your reviewers graciously for their consideration. If you can get some advance reviews by notable people in photography, or even experts on the theme of your photography, then you will want to print those reviews on the cover of your book, and use them in all of your marketing materials. For cover/jacket blurbs, providing a pdf file of the book and cover will suffice.

Of course, you can still try sending your final bound books out for review to some publications, but simply not the big reviewers. Think creatively as to whom you can approach and research which publications don't require the pre-publication copies and the four-month lead time.

9.  Three months before publication, create a website for your book. If you can, have the domain name match the name of your book title. Include a blog on your website that you update regularly. Include news, tips, and information about photography. Think of ways to create a following with your readers—you want them to keep coming back. You can also sell your photographs on the site. Create an ongoing relationship with people, make a connection, and not only will they return—they will tell other people about you.

10. Design and produce color postcards and bookmarks to promote your book. Modern Postcard is a great company to use for this; they have inexpensive packages, quality printing, and fast turnaround.

*A QR code that links to Amazon's Advantage Program, enabling you to sell your book on Amazon.com. http://tinyurl.com/yalnram*

*A QR code that links to Barnes and Noble's submission process to make your book available for order through their online bookstore and retail stores. http://tinyurl.com/3b7zq4*

11. Begin taking some of your prepublication review copies to local independent bookstores, photography stores, and retail establishments. Ask to meet with the manager and give each one with whom you meet a copy of the book and any postcards or sales material you have created. Request that they consider selling your book in their store. Get your book into as many local establishments as you can. Research other independent bookstores outside of your city but within your region of the country where it would be easy to drive to in a day. Some of these bookstores might even be agreeable to hosting a book signing once your book is published.

12. Go the Amazon.com website, scroll to the bottom until you see "Make Money with Us." Below that is an arrow beside the words "See all." Select that and on the next page you'll see "Amazon Advantage." This is where you apply to sell your book. Barnes and Noble also has an online bookstore, but you must go through a review process first. Go to their main website, click on "Our Company" and on the next page, on the top menu bar, select "For Authors." This is where you can apply.

13. Begin planning a book party where you can launch your book and sign copies. Create an email blast to advertise the event using that database you built. Do you have gallery representation for your photography? If so, have a book-signing event along with an exhibit of your work.

14. Send a press kit to the local newspapers, neighborhood newspapers, art magazines, city magazines, and your local NPR station. Try to get some of them to write a news story on you and your upcoming book. If the theme of your photography book corresponds with a community, social, or environmental issue, someone from the publication might interview you and then write or talk about your book. You'll want to create a press kit in print form as well as digital. Start with a folder that contains a well-written press release. You also want to include your bio as well as advance book reviews and quotes from peers and professionals praising your photography and the book. Insert a few of your best photographs

that appear in the book, as well as a computer disk containing high-resolution files for use in articles and reviews.

You'll also want to create an online press kit you can keep on your website with downloadable high-resolution images that the media can have access to. When you do email blasts to the media, you should include a link to your online press kit with all necessary instructions on how to access it.

Now let's review the structure of your marketing plan and the information it should contain. Your plan must be professionally typed with the following pages:

- TITLE PAGE
  This should include the title of your book, the author's name, the words "Proposal for Marketing," and your contact information.
- TABLE OF CONTENTS
  This should list all the sections and pages included in the proposal.
- INTRODUCTION
  This is a one-page book summary with a final sentence that states how the plan outlines the procedures for marketing and promoting the book.
- PUBLISHING TEAM
  This page lists the author, designer, editor, publicist, sales and marketing manager—anyone involved with the creation and promotion of your book.
- STRATEGIES
  This should state who your main target market is, as well as any secondary target markets. Then create a list of all the strategies on how you plan to reach them.
- MARKETING PLAN DETAILS
  This will be several pages long and should include specifics listed like this:
  *Press kit*
  - press release
  - book excerpts for use in publications

- biography of author
- endorsements from notable photographers, critics, readers
- brochures, postcards, fliers
- promotional copies of book
- author Q & A

*Book signings and readings*
- begin in your local area and expand
- formulate lists to target:
  - independent bookstores
  - galleries
  - photography clubs and associations
  - organizations matching the theme of your photography

*Review submissions*
- Make a list of each place you plan to send prepublication review copies. (*The New York Times Book Review, photo-eye Magazine, Photo District News* magazine, etc.)

*Announcement campaigns*
- This step details the various methods you should use to announce the publication of your book:
  - create database of potential buyers
  - announce book availability, include teaser ad, note upcoming signing/reading/interview, events, etc.
  - email blast ad campaign
  - website and Facebook campaign

*Marketing*
- Make a list of other sales venues, photo magazines, galleries, etc.

*Award submissions*
- List each award submission separately and describe it as a partial list.

*Collaboration with nonprofit sector*

  – If the theme of your book has any connection with a nonprofit cause, make a list here of each organization and how you plan to collaborate with them, for example, offering a percentage of proceeds from book sales, maintaining membership, and participating in discussions, etc.)

*Interactive website*

  (This should list everything you plan do with your website to generate traffic, make connections with viewers, and build a following.)

  – Overview of the book

  – Author biography

  – Book reviews

  – Blog to share stories, photographs, book tour, events

  – Book transaction option or link through site

  – Resources section

· SCHEDULE

This section should start with a sentence similar to this: *Author is available for all travel, book signings, events, and interviews. Scheduling is tentative due to negotiations regarding printing and delivery of books.* The schedule should list dates alongside the following:

  – Prepublication review copies sent to media.

  – First email blast campaign begins.

  – Mail postcard announcements.

  – Blog on the book's website is live.

  – Begin scheduling events.

  – Visit bookstores and other retail establishments.

  – Connect with related nonprofits and other organizations.

  – Publication date for book.

  – Publication parties and appearances.

  – Submit book to award competitions.

## Marketing Budget

This should include all costs associated with executing the marketing plan—even postage! Get at least three quotes from vendors for everything you plan to print, create, cater, and mail. Even if you do the design yourself, enter the cost of how much you would have to pay if you had contracted that out. The item list should look similar to this one, but you will want to insert your quantities and costs and delete my placeholders:

| | |
|---|---:|
| — Fifty prepublication review copies | $ 1,000 |
| — Design of postcard announcements | 350 |
| — One thousand postcard announcements | 500 |
| — Email blast advertising campaign | 900 |
| — Website development: | |
|     Hosting | 150 |
|     Domain purchase and maintenance fee | 50 |
|     Design and information maintenance | 4,000 |
| — Book signings and events: | |
|     Transportation and accommodations | 2,500 |
| — Sell sheets, fliers, brochures | |
|     Two thousand with postage | 3,000 |
| — Publication parties: | |
|     Invitations: four hundred | 400 |
|     Catering services and supplies | 1,500 |
| — Promotional book postage | 500 |
| — Awards and review entry/consideration fees | 700 |

| | |
|---|---:|
| TOTAL: | $15,550 |

DON'T PANIC when you look at that total! Remember, as a creative and talented person, you may be doing a lot of the design, website development, writing, and catering yourself. These prices reflect what it would cost to hire people for those tasks. Even if you supply the sweat equity, you want to show intent and commitment to anyone with whom you share this proposal. Need printing? Find local companies to barter with and offer your services in payment for printing. Need a book event? Have your friends throw a huge book party! Think outside the box.

For more marketing ideas, you should sign up for John Kremer's weekly book marketing tips. The tips are sent by email, they are free, and they are very helpful. Not only will you learn more about marketing your book, you will be invited to join webinars, seminars, review lists of retail shops and bookstores that will stock self-published books, read the experiences of other authors, find names of printers, distributors and too many other resources to mention. He offers a wealth of information, and I highly recommend you sign on: www.bookmarket.com/tips.htm. Here is a QR code linked to his website. He also has a book you should consider reading, *1001 Ways to Market Your Books*. While it's not targeted to photography books specifically, you will be amazed at how you can apply so many of the ideas and suggestions to your own marketing efforts.

Join some photography book groups where you can share, promote your work, and learn about the work of other photographers. Photography books are hot now! Many articles have recently been written about their increasing investment value as a collector's item. Digital books are finding their place among mass market novels, how-to books, and educational books, which appears to be making fine art and photography books even more exclusive. I believe this trend will continue because photography books are art in themselves, something you can touch, hold, and collect.

One of my favorite online photography book groups is Flak Photo Books on Facebook. The group is hosted by Andy Adams of AndyAdamsPhoto.com and FlakPhoto.com. He is a digital producer and photo publisher who's mission is promoting photography and photography books on a global level as well as connecting other photographers and fostering supportive online social media collaboration. It's a great forum, and I highly recommend you join: http://facebook.com/FlakPhotoBooks. Here is a QR code and a link to the Facebook group. If you decide to join, send a request on the site and Andy will accept you as a member.

You should also familiarize yourself with the Indie Photobook Library founded by Larissa Leclair in Washington DC. The archive is an exquisite collection of over 1,000 photography books from small independent presses and self-published authors around the world. Selections from the archive are regularly curated for special exhibits, but you can also visit the Library to view and handle the books. Here is a QR code and a link to the website: http://www.indiephotobooklibrary.org/.

*". . . the Indie Photobook Library is fast becoming one of Washington's more interesting small collections."*

—Mark Jenkins,
*Washington Post Express*
November 9, 2011

You should also clear your schedule each October for the Atlanta Celebrates Photography (ACP) Book Fair. ACP sponsors events all year, but in October the city of Atlanta becomes a photography mecca and one of the best events is the ACP Book Fair. You can connect with other photographers who have published their own books and if your book is published you can sell it there as well. A short list of other photography book festivals worth attending include: the CODEX International Book Fair, the Decatur Book Festival, Editions|Artists Book Fair, the Indie and Small Press Book Fair, the Kasseler Photobook-Festival, the London Art Book Fair, the New York Art Book Fair, and the San Francisco Book Festival. Check them out online for locations and dates.

Last, please keep in mind that what I've offered to you in this section, is simply an example of what to include in your marketing plan and how to structure it. Every book is different, so you should customize it for your own needs using this as your guide. Most importantly, don't let yourself feel overwhelmed by the marketing. Structure it in a way that will work for you for and sell those books!

## STORAGE, DISTRIBUTION, AND FULFILLMENT

Are you relaxing now, contemplating which pen to use when you begin autographing all those books? An extra-fine point "Sharpie" is best, and, personally, I prefer blue! But let's not get ahead of ourselves; you've still got to decide where to store all those books when they arrive and how to get them to your adoring fans—even for those who don't know they adore you yet!

In the last section, we addressed the role of a book distributor mainly for the purpose of creating your marketing plan and budget if you are self-publishing. Even if you don't want to use a distributor, it's important for you to know what it is early in the process so that you can thoughtfully eliminate it from your plans if you choose to. If you have a conventional publisher, they will arrange getting your book into retail outlets, Amazon, and bookstores through their wholesale or distribution channels.

If you are publishing with a POD company, most sales will come from your targeted personal efforts, and you can expect a few random sales from the POD online bookstore. Blurb has a blog forum where users can openly discuss the quantity of books they have sold through Blurb's online bookstore and quite a few identify themselves as photographers and artists. On a recent visit to their forum, I noted most people sold between zero and twenty copies, one person sold thirty, one person sold fifty and another eighty-one. Several mentioned that they had greater sales success by having the books shipped directly to them where they placed them into their local independent bookstores and retail shops.

Blurb doesn't offer distribution outside of their online bookstore. If you use Blurb and want to sell books on Amazon, you will need to have books shipped to you, establish your account with Amazon's Advantage program, and send them books as needed to maintain their inventory. Some of the other POD companies have limited distribution through Amazon and wholesalers, but these services are not like those you would find with a distributor. What's the difference? I'll explain in a moment.

If you are self-publishing using offset printing, I'm not convinced that hiring a distributor is appropriate for your book because photography books are definitely a niche market and perhaps not worth the effort and cost. You would need to have a specific "hook" that would make your photography book commercially appealing to the masses, and most don't. The majority of photography books are truly a very small part of the book market. If distributors may not be a wise choice, what about wholesalers and fulfillment companies? What do they do?

Let's define them, compare their services, and take a look at how they charge for them.

BOOK DISTRIBUTOR: This is a company who represents you and your book to book-sellers using sales materials and book catalogs. Some distributors will offer optional fee-based marketing services in addition to their standard distribution contract. But basically, it's your job to inform consumers that your book exists and convince them they want and need it. After that, the distributor makes it available to them for purchase. They require exclusive representation of your book, and, in return, they warehouse the books, sell them, process orders, ship books to stores, and process returns. Most distributors require that you be an established publisher, which means you have at least ten titles already in print, or you have other books in the wings, or that your current book will be part of a series. If you have less than ten books, then you are an emerging publisher or a self-publisher, and while they are fewer in number, there are distributors who specialize in distribution for one to nine titles. And other than programs directly associated with POD companies, book distributors will not accept POD titles.

How do distributors make their money? When a book sells, they either pay you a percentage of the list price (retail price), which might be 40 percent or they charge a percentage of net sales (after discounts to bookstores) which ranges from 25 to 29 percent. Bookstores typically get a 45 to 50 percent discount off the list price so both you and distributor yield a very small percentage. In order for the distributors to maintain a stream of income, they have to sell many books on a regular basis, which is why they don't like representing only one title from a publisher.

As an example, let's say your book is priced at $29.95, and the distributor negotiates to pay you 40 percent of that list price. They sell it to the bookstore at a 50% discount which is $14.98. The book is sold to a store, you get $11.98, and the distributor gets $2.99. However, if the distributor contracts to charge you 25 percent of net sales, then you only receive $11.23, and they get $3.75. If they sell to a wholesaler rather than a bookstore, the wholesaler typically gets a discount of about 55 percent so you both yield even less.

That's not a lot to get paid for your book, is it? There are other charges as well. The distributor must pack and ship the books to stores, which is charged back to you. They need to cover the cost of returns as well. If a book doesn't sell in a bookstore, they can return it to the distributor for a refund. The distributor needs to handle and process that transaction. For this they may charge between 5–9 percent. It all adds up quickly, doesn't it?

WHOLESALER: This is a company that buys books directly from publishers at an even steeper discount than bookstores do. Expect it to be around 55 percent, though it will vary depending on the company. The wholesalers stock the books in huge warehouses and sell them to stores at a lower discount and then pocket the rest. It's simple, as there are no other fees. They don't represent you; they represent the stores that they sell to. Wholesalers will buy from publishing companies but not necessarily from a self-published author. There are also a few companies who are labeled wholesalers but who act more like fulfillment houses.

FULFILLMENT HOUSE: Standard fulfillment houses do not buy books from you, and they do not attempt to sell your books to bookstores or retail establishments. They will warehouse your books, accept orders from customers, and pack and ship the books. They offer no sales materials or marketing options, and therefore they do not require any exclusive representation contract. They make their money typically by charging per month for warehousing the books, the cost of processing orders, and packaging and shipping them out. The rates and terms can vary greatly depending on the size, weight, and number of books you have. One company might charge $195 per month plus $2.50 to process an order. Another might charge $12 per full pallet (skid) per month and then a percentage of the list price to process and ship. It can get expensive and probably will offer you similar profits that a distributor would.

Some wholesalers perform more like fulfillment houses, and many POD companies have relationships with them. When a POD company tells you to expect distribution services through them, it's not the same as the distributors we first defined on page 74. POD companies, some of which were born from mother companies like Ingram and Amazon, have established vehicles to process orders for POD books. They really function more like fulfillment companies. So don't think your POD book is being peddled to a major bookstore buyer as the next hot item they should stock on their shelves, because that would truly misrepresent their services. I'm not criticizing the POD company claims; I'm simply saying, let's define what their term "distribution" means. If you speak with a POD company who tells you otherwise, ask for specifics and get proof of what they are promising.

You can see how having a distributor or fulfillment house frees up your living space as well as your time, but it will cut into your profits and you should be aware of that. So what's the alternative? You could do it yourself. For storage, you will need a dry, temperature controlled environment because books cannot endure extreme temperatures or they will mildew and warp. Here are some ideas to consider:

- an area of your basement that is dry with temperatures that are in the 50 to 75 degree range, and with about 50 percent humidity. Some references will tell you 60 to 70 degrees, but my experience of working in a publishing company with its own warehouse showed me that books are typically safely stored in temperatures ranging a little outside of that.
- a spare bedroom or office
- a temperature-controlled storage space
- a room or space in your office building where you could pay a monthly fee for storage
- a room at a friend's house where you could pay a storage fee
- a section of a warehouse belonging to a printer you have a relationship with for a monthly storage fee, or barter with them for your design and photography skills.

Once you secure a space for the books, think about how you will handle processing orders and shipping books. If you have sporadic orders, this shouldn't be a big deal. But that's not what you want—you want books to fly off the shelves! With all of your aggressive marketing efforts, you want to be overwhelmed with orders! If that happens, and you cannot manage on your own, think about relatives or friends you could pull in to assist you either with the shipping or bookkeeping. If you have an established photography business then perhaps an assistant can help you and you can increase their compensation for the additional tasks added to their responsibilities. What about a student who needs some extra cash? Brainstorm some ideas, and you'll come up with a few solutions to explore that will keep more of the money from book sales in your pocket rather than building the profits of another company.

If you have your own photography business, then you are already familiar with the procedures of making a sale. If not, then you need to be aware that as you will be selling a product, you need to charge sales tax in order to be in compliance with your state government tax laws. If you don't already have a sales tax number, you will need to contact your state department of revenue to apply for one. Once you receive it, you will charge sales tax on each final sale you make. Sales taxes are only charged on final sales to end-users. Periodically throughout the year, you will be required to prepare a report and pay the sales tax you collected.

In addition to regular check payments, many people use PayPal to process orders. But accepting credit cards is another great option for added flexibility of payment. If you have an iPhone, Droid, or similar Smartphone, you can now easily accept credit payments in person using your phone. It can be done on the phone itself by inputting information, or you can get a small swipe attachment that allows you to actually swipe the credit card enabling the information to be automatically processed. Then your customer signs his or her name with a fingertip to complete the transaction. It's a very simple process, and several companies offer this service, including Intuit for Droid phones and Square App for the iPhone.

Having various methods of accepting payment will also be helpful when you begin selling your photographic prints.

Eliot Dudik is a fine art photographer. His book, *Road Ends in Water*, was published in 2010. To see more of his work, visit his website: www.EliotDudik.com.

To see the full multimedia interview with Eliot, as well as interviews with other photographers, go to www.HowtoPublishYourOwnPhotographyBook.com or scan this QR code with your smartphone.

A CONVERSATION WITH *Eliot Dudik*

**WHEN DID YOUR INTEREST IN PHOTOGRAPHY FIRST BEGIN?**
I first discovered photography when I was attending high school near Baltimore. I went on to pursue degrees in art history and anthropology at College of Charleston as a foundation for my photography.

**WHAT PHOTOGRAPHERS HAVE INFLUENCED YOU THE MOST?**
Joel Sternfeld, Alec Soth, Robert Adams, Stephen Shore, Richard Misrach, William Eggleston, and William Christenberry.

**HOW DID YOU DECIDE ON THE SUBJECT MATTER FOR YOUR FIRST BOOK?**
I worked part-time at a cigar/martini bar while attending College of Charleston, It was there that I met several locals who lived in the area and shared their stories about South Carolina history. A few years after graduating, I moved to Savannah, Georgia, to work toward a Masters of Fine Art degree in photography at Savannah College of Art and Design. I found that I really missed Charleston, so I drove back there to live on weekends. It was through all of this that I came to document the deep connection between the landscape and people of the coastal region of southern Carolina.

**WHAT DO YOU WANT TO COMMUNICATE WITH THIS BODY OF WORK?**
A sense of place, first and foremost. Through that sense of place, I hope those who view the

photographs find an appreciation for the land and the folks who live there.

**WHY DID YOU CHOOSE TO SELF-PUBLISH YOUR BOOK?**

I self-published the book because it granted me the greatest freedom throughout the publishing process and after.

**HOW DID YOU GO ABOUT EDITING YOUR IMAGES AND CREATING A SEQUENCE IN THE BOOK?**

I began with several working edits, and after setting a concrete "stop shooting day," I edited everything I had shot over a year and a half down to about seventy-five photographs. I then made seven copies of each of the seventy-five images as 4" x 5" prints. I passed out the sets to the folks I trust the most to get their interpretations of an edit. I then charted out each person's edit on a large board with all the thumbnails of the images, placing color-coded stars next to the thumbnails that corresponded to particular people's choices. I used the chart as a guide and to reassure many of my own choices. The edit was then down to about forty-five images. Those photographs were then printed at about 8" x 10" and hung on a long continuous wall. Every day for about two weeks, I looked at the images on the wall and moved them around, adding and subtracting images as needed. Once satisfied, I taped 4" x 5" images of the sequence

11" x 8.5" trim size with 96 pages
Paper stock: 100 pound gloss
Perfect bound with soft cover
Flood matte lamination on cover
Ink: CMYK 4/color process cover and interior

Self-published with a 1,000 book print run
Printed and bound in Iceland at Oddi
 Printing Corporation
Photographs taken with large format camera
List price: $29.95

into a blank book, along with cut out captions and other accompanying texts, to determine if the sequence progressed the way it was intended to within a book. I finally settled on the thirty-nine-image edit and sequence published in the book, and it was time to consult with my graphic designer.

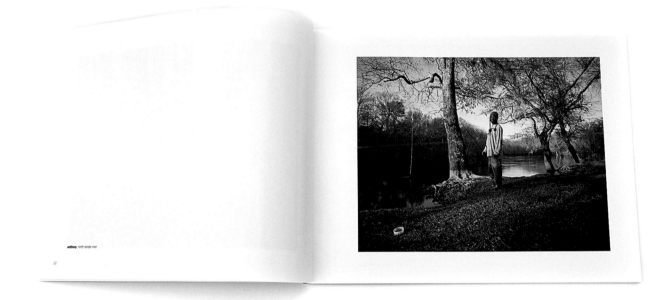

anthony, north edisto river

20

**DID YOU CONSULT WITH ANY PHOTOGRAPHERS OR CURATORS FOR ASSISTANCE WITH THE BOOK?**
I was fortunate enough to have a number of photographers and photographic educators I turned to for assistance with the editing and sequencing process.

**DID YOU HIRE A DESIGNER, OR DID YOU DESIGN THE BOOK YOURSELF?**
I hired an excellent designer named Steve Acres to design the book. He and I worked very closely to arrive at the final design and layout. I have some experience in design, and design most everything else myself, but I left the book and my website to Steve as he is the expert and clearly knows more than I.

**HOW DID YOU CHOOSE YOUR DESIGNER?**
I met Steve Acres at a Savannah College of Art and Design event where they were showcasing some of the best MFA work in the photography and graphic design programs. He was exhibiting some of his work, which I was immediately drawn to. We struck up a conversation, and discussed my book project. He was easy to work with from the beginning, listening carefully to what I envisioned.

**HOW LONG DID YOU WORK ON THE BOOK BEFORE IT WAS PUBLISHED?**
I photographed for the project during the year and a half I was in graduate school, and I researched self-publishing, graphic designers, printing companies, papers, cover stocks, varnishes, bindings, distribution, etc., the entire year and half as well. It was published to correspond with the completion of my thesis and first exhibition of these photographs.

**DO YOU HAVE A DISTRIBUTOR FOR YOUR BOOK AND, IF SO, WHO IS IT?**
I do not use a distributor. I distribute the books myself to bookstores locally and

A CONVERSATION WITH *Eliot Dudik*

80

around the world, including photo-eye in Santa Fe, New Mexico and Beyond Words in Scotland. Most of my books are sold from my website (www.eliotdudik.com), and I ship them out myself.

DID YOU DEVELOP A MARKETING PLAN AND BUDGET FOR THE BOOK?
The marketing plan and budget were things I worked on during that year and a half in graduate school, prior to publication.

DID YOU WORK WITH ANY PUBLICISTS AND, IF SO, HOW DID YOU FIND THEM?
I did not work with any publicists, although the *Road Ends in Water* series received a good deal of attention through publication and press from *Fraction Magazine*;, *F-Stop Magazine*; *Magenta Magazine*; Flak Photo; *The Great Leap Sideways*; *Ahorn Magazine*; *Lenscratch*; *PDN*; *One, One Thousand: A Publication of Southern Photography*; B&H; and Fall Line Press. I owe the recognition this work has received to these organizations, and many others, as well as several exhibitions across the country.

WHAT WAS THE COST OF PRODUCING THE BOOK?
The printing and binding costs came to $10,000.

WHY DID YOU CHOOSE A BOOK AS A WAY TO SHARE YOUR PHOTOGRAPHY?
I chose to produce a book because of its inherent narrative qualities and intimate nature. I was also interested in its potential to reach a large audience.

HOW HAS THIS BOOK HELPED YOU AS AN ARTIST?
The book has certainly surpassed my goals in reaching a wide audience, having shipped it all over the world. It has been an excellent marketing tool to progress my career as a photographer and educator, and has given me the opportunity to discuss my photographic and publishing experience at a number of venues.

WHAT ADVICE DO YOU HAVE FOR OTHER PHOTOGRAPHERS WHO WANT TO PUBLISH THEIR BOOK?
Do your research on the front end. Use your research to know what you want and why you want it. Look for advice from friends, colleagues, peers, and other professionals in the field. Expect a lot of hard work, both before and after the book is published, and in so doing, expect a rewarding experience.

WHAT ARE YOU WORKING ON NOW?
While teaching at the University of South Carolina, I have been traveling

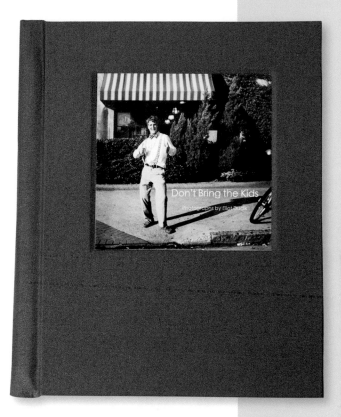

and working on a new series of images from around the state. I also recently finished a small series of handmade books from an ongoing project I started about the madness of Saint Patrick's Day in Savannah, Georgia. That book is titled, *Don't Bring the Kids*.

# THE BOOK

## PUBLICITY, PROMOTIONS, AND SOCIAL MEDIA

### ERRATUM AND CORRIGENDUM

*Erratum is a single correction of a production error in a book noted after the book is already printed and bound, but before it is made available to sell. Errata is a list of errors and corrections. I've read that some people use the word corrigenda if it's an author error, though I've found errata and corrigenda used interchangeably, with corrigendum referring to a list of errors.*

*The method of communicating the correction is typically a sheet of paper inserted into the book noting the error and the correction. Most errors do not warrant this, it's not uncommon to find a misspelling or other small errors in a book. However, if it is a serious mistake, or one that would cause confusion, then that is the way to handle it.*

*If it's a an error that you cannot live with, then for considerable expense, you can utilize the services of a book repair company who can use tip-ins and other methods to correct the error. You can find the names of them in the resources section of this book.*

Your book has finally arrived! What a feeling it is to hold it in your hands, to turn each page as it reveals a story of your experience and your journey. Somewhere during the process, did you feel that the book began to take on a life of its own? That's always my experience, and I find it quite thrilling to create something that didn't exist before in a form that other people can share in and perhaps even be changed by. How many eyes will pass over the pages of your book—this tiny bit of your legacy?

I will briefly bring up a subject that I hope none of you will ever have to deal with. What happens if you receive your book, you open it, and, to your horror, discover an error that you missed in all the previous proofs? First, you should know that almost every book published will contain some minor error whether it be an extra space, a misplaced comma, or even a misspelling. We are human, and even with all of our checks and balances, many times, small errors will still slip through our careful proofreading process. With these small errors, you simply have to take a deep breath and then let it go. Most people will not notice it. However, if it's a glaring error in a very prominent place that you simply cannot live with, there are specialty companies that can do some level of book correction whether it be a sticker or a tipped-in page. One source is Dunn and Company in Massachusetts. Their website name says it all: www.booktrauma.com. Another company, NuDea, is located in Kentucky. Both companies are listed in the resources section in the back of this book, though I hope you never need to contact them. Repairs at this point can be very costly, so you should get cost estimates and then decide if the error is serious enough to warrant that level of expenditure. Also, think creatively; is there another way to artistically deal with the error and perhaps turn it into a positive? Give it considerable thought before taking action. Do not make a decision from an emotional place. Discreetly ask for feedback from a few trusted peers, and be as objective as possible.

By now, if you've followed your publishing schedule, your promotions plan is well underway and potential buyers are anxiously awaiting the arrival of your book. Where should you be at this point in your promotions plan?

- Email blasts have all been sent out.
- Postcards announcing your book should have been mailed.
- You should have some book reviews from all of your review requests and, if you haven't already done it, add the best of them to your book's website.
- Your account with Amazon is established, and you can now send the first shipment of books to them.
- If they haven't already, Barnes and Noble should be contacting you with their decision as to whether they will list your book on their online bookstore. Check the status of that now.
- Confirm that any other online bookstores you contracted with are ready to receive book shipments.
- Your book's website should be live, with your blog actively updating your readers about the arrival of your book, including a book launch and book signings.
- Now is the perfect time to reconnect with those bookstores you approached about carrying your books. Some may purchase a few copies, while others will choose to stock your book on consignment. Be flexible and work with the manager or owner so that it's beneficial to both of you. Regardless of your contact's initial decision, be sure to give them a copy of your book along with a marketing sheet containing reviews and any articles that have been written about you and your book. You may get a call back!
- How many book signings do you have scheduled? You should have several spread all over town and several in surrounding cities as well. You should have lists of these bookstores all over your region of the country. Network and keep scheduling them over the next six to twelve months. If your photography focuses on a specific geographic region other than where you live, then you should be networking there, too.

## FEE-BASED PROMOTIONS PAY OFF FOR EVERYONE!

*A recent trend that began with the Boulder Book Store in Boulder, Colorado, is a fee-based program for stocking self-published books. The store's head buyer found that so many self-published authors were wanting their books in the store that it began to consume too much of their administrative time to put the titles in the inventory system, stock the books, and manage each one. But they truly wanted to support the local authors and offer them ways to promote their book just as the large publishers do.*

*So they launched a fee-based program, through which, for a handling fee of $25, you can have your self-published book in their bookstore. You can also pay for additional services such as premium display placement in their store, on their website, and book signings. The program has been so successful that other bookstores around the country have begun copying or adapting the program to fit their needs.*

*The result? Self-published authors who have a high-quality book, and have marketed heavily to create a demand for it—are selling books, and often-times—lots of books! So, if you encounter a bookstore owner who hesitates in stocking your book, consider suggesting this type of an arrangement!*

- You should be on the schedule of photography organizations and clubs all over your city and surrounding areas. Plan to speak to these groups about your photography and your book. Present a slide show of your work, and then sell your book to people in attendance.
- Follow up with your media contacts and send each of them a copy of the book. Do not be shy. You need to reconnect with whomever you made contact with during your preliminary marketing and promotions push. Sharing the unveiling of your hard work may be just the reminder and push they need to follow through on that article they had planned to write or the radio interview where they wanted you to talk about your book and photography.
- Send a copy of your book to whomever wrote your introduction and to anyone else who helped in the production and creation of your book. Don't forget to also send a copy, as required, to the Library of Congress.
- What about organizations and nonprofits that have a theme or interest that relates to your photography? Did they agree to purchase any books or sell them on their website? Follow up with all of these organizations and give them copies of your book.
- If you don't already have one, you should establish a Facebook page specifically for your book. There you can make book announcements and link them to your book's website, book blog, YouTube book trailer, and Twitter stream.

YouTube book trailer? Yes, that's right, but I'll get to that a little later. Social media can and should play a very significant role in the marketing and promotions of your book. Facebook currently has over 900 million active users. Take advantage of the millions of people you can potentially reach by creating a viral following of your book through social media. For many years, Facebook has a feature where you can "Like" a product, service, company, or person who is a member of Facebook. Once you get your book's Facebook page created, you need to encourage everyone you can to click that "Like" button in order to promote and create a viral explosion of interest in your book! If you are familiar with Facebook, you already know how to create your own page. You may or may not know how to add another page within your existing account, but it's very easy. Go to www.Facebook.com/pages/create.php. You will see these options and instructions:

Create a Page for a:

Local Business or Place

Company, Organization or Institution

Brand or Product (*select this one*)

Artist, Band, or Public Figure

Entertainment

Cause or Community

Now you can customize your book page with photos of the cover and interior spreads just as you had set up your personal Facebook page. Include book reviews, a summary about the book, and all of your upcoming book events and signings. You can also import your book blog into Facebook to expand exposure for your book. To import your blog into Facebook, go this link: https://apps.facebook.com/rssgraffiti/, or scan this QR code.

This is an app, so you will need to authorize it and follow the instructions. You should be prompted to paste in the URL of your RSS feed. Once you complete that, your blog should load into Facebook and update it automatically when you add new entries.

Your goal now is to attract people and build a following for your book page and blog. If your friends are fans of your book and want to support you further, ask them to share your blog with their friends, and it will create even greater exposure for your book. You can also explore paying for an ad on Facebook, but I suspect that might end up being too costly

## WHAT ARE RSS AND ATOM FEED?

*Both RSS and Atom are XML language formats specifically for news, audio, video, and blogs that are frequently updated for syndication. The resulting document itself is called a feed, web feed, or channel.*

## HOW CAN YOU FIND YOUR RSS OR ATOM FEED URL?

*If you have installed an RSS feed icon, you can click on* 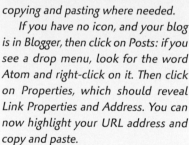 *that to reveal the URL for copying and pasting where needed.*

*If you have no icon, and your blog is in Blogger, then click on Posts: if you see a drop menu, look for the word Atom and right-click on it. Then click on Properties, which should reveal Link Properties and Address. You can now highlight your URL address and copy and paste.*

*If this doesn't work, right-click on Atom and select Send Link. Your RSS feed URL should load into your mail program where you can copy it there.*

*In Wordpress, you may see the letters RSS, and if you click on them, it will take you to your RSS feed URL. If not, type /feed to the end of your blog URL, and it should take you there.*

*In tumblr you can add /rss to the end of your blog URL, and it will take you to your RSS feed.*

an endeavor for most authors, and, from what I've read, I'm not convinced the return is worth the cost.

Focus instead on other ways to increase traffic to your website, your blog, and your book's Facebook page. Once you begin getting people interested in your book and your blog, you must keep them coming by blogging regularly (daily if you can), replying to comments and making connections, creating more content, news (related to your area of photography), and resources that will add value for them.

Two other great social media tools for you to consider are YouTube and Vimeo. Increasingly, authors are creating book trailers to introduce and promote their new books—even well-known authors have book trailers now. The key to this being effective is to make a high-quality trailer. You'll see a LOT of bad book trailers out there, so if you plan to do this, do it right. Let's look at some good book trailers for photography books. You'll be able to see the level of quality and how the approach to creating them is perfectly customized to the theme of their book. Use the accompanying QR code with your smartphone to access these or check out the links on your computer:

Ryan Adams, *Ryan Adams & the Cardinals: A View of Other Windows*
http://bit.ly/J5f9Hi (1 min. 23 seconds)

Mary Ellen Mark, *Prom*
http://bit.ly/ytfSny (1 min. 33 seconds)

Uwe Skrczypczak, *Wildlife Photography*
http://www.youtube.com/watch?v=fg4SbTbtxDo  (60 seconds)

Scott Pasfield, *Gay in America*
http://www.youtube.com/watch?v=5S1emYtI8_E  (1 min. 57 seconds)

As you view these trailers, take note of the background music, graphics, and various techniques for transitioning from one frame to the next. These trailers range in length from 60 seconds to 1 minutes, 57 seconds. Personally I think 1 minute and 30 seconds is ideal; it allows enough time to get your message across without losing the attention of the viewer. Note that a couple of these examples were created by publishing companies with a budget to professionally produce them. But don't let that deter you from using these as a model to create your own book trailer. With the video capability your DSLR camera has, you can create a very nice video with simple props, some still photographs, and perhaps some background music. You can use the sound recording on your camera, but for better quality, I recommend you purchase a digital recorder such as Zoom, as well as a Lavalier mic for interviews. If your budget won't stretch to include these, then you can use your camera's sound, but—the better quality sound will go a long way toward presenting a compelling and professional book trailer.

In addition to the techniques used in the book trailers I've included here as examples, a photography book could also lend itself to an interview setting with simple background music. The camera can focus on you, the author, with either questions heard from someone off-camera or a simple dialogue between the interviewer and you, the author.

The camera could also focus on you simply talking about your career and why you chose to publish the book. As you speak, the camera can transition from you to still photographs and back to you. You could include a cover of your book at the beginning or end of the trailer, or both. Reviews are important, too, so try to find a way to include them tastefully. This is just one approach; create a storyboard sketch of your ideas until you find one that you like best. Look at other photography book trailers. Examine how they begin, what audio they use, how they frame their images, what transition techniques are used, and how they end with a call of action to purchase. Make notes on which trailers you like and why, do the same with trailers you don't like. It will help you as you create and edit yours.

Keep in mind that there may be copyright ownership issues with specific music you would like to use, so you should either find something in public domain, pay a small fee for something you like, or work with a musician with whom you could barter for the music. You can easily find a young film student to assist you with the filming or, again, barter with a local videographer in town. You can do this without spending a small fortune, and the end result is a powerful promotions tool that you can place on your website and on DVDs you provide to potential stores. In fact, you could even include this in a digital press kit!

Your video should also be posted on your book's website, your book's Facebook page, Vimeo, and other social media venues. Do your research though, because videos need to be created, saved, and exported to very precise formats to work with different venues. If you plan to provide video that might even be used for broadcast on a television station, then I recommend you hire a professional videographer to create your trailer so that they shoot it correctly and export it in the correct formats you'll need. If you're serious about doing this yourself with an assistant, then at least take a video class and a post-production class to learn how to produce them correctly and export them in the correct formats that media will require.

Don't forget about Twitter, which now is even being used by the editors of large publishing companies. You should do the same. It's a brilliant platform that you can use to network and build a following for your book.

Why is this necessary when you already have a website and Facebook page? Isn't that enough? Even within your specific target market, there is a percentage of the public who visit Facebook regularly. Other people will use search engines and look for websites. People from another percentage of your market are using Twitter. The more methods you use to attract people using all of these different forms of communication, the quicker you will build a following of fans.

Once you have your Twitter account, you can also link it to your Facebook so your Twitter stream is transferred there, too. How does Twitter work? It's a networking service accessed from your computer or phone where you receive and send messages with a maximum of 140 characters. Each message is called a Tweet, and they appear on your Twitter home page.

1.  Make a connection with others by doing searches on Twitter for people who are involved in photography, who own independent bookstores or galleries, or who are interested in the theme of your book. You can even connect with book reviewers.

    – Once on Twitter, at the top menu bar, click on "Discover." In the left column, click on "Find friends" or "Browse categories," and select anyone or anything that might be a good match for your book, or might have followers who would be a match for your book.

2.  When you find people that your book is suited for, start to "follow" them, spend some time reading their Tweets. Listen first, and then reach out!

3.  Send those people a Tweet asking about their store, photography, or interests. Respond to their Tweets and take note of other people following them. Once you make a connection they may start following you, which increases your exposure. They key here is to build relationships.

4.  One thing to keep in mind about messages you send using Twitter: the Tweets should contain approximately 90 percent content and 10 percent product promotion. It should not be obvious that you want to promote your book; that will come naturally as a result of your networking with other people who have similar interests. You must be genuine.

5.  So what should you Tweet about? You can Tweet about your photographic process, offer links that contain great resources in photography, links that correspond to issues around the theme of your photography, etc. You can Tweet a little about your personal life, but try and keep it focused on information you can offer to help others and gain visibility in the process. Tweet with links to your ongoing blog. In this way, you're sharing original content that is of interest to readers, and they'll see your book for sale on your blog site so that creates an opportunity for purchase.

6.  Follow others and take note of the things they Tweet about. It will help you to see how the process works. Book agents Tweet and even Abrams' editors Tweet. You can check them out on Twitter: @ABRAMSBooks.

It's important that you open your Twitter account and begin tweeting as soon as possible. It takes time to develop a following, and you want a lot of followers by the time your book is published.

I try to Tweet every day or two and have found that I average about one hundred new followers each month. I don't follow everyone who follows me because there are spammers out there and followers who really aren't related to my topic. Many people will drop you if you don't follow them back. The key is to have quality followers who will retweet your tweets to their followers, thereby expanding your exposure.

The latest statistics show that 140 million people use Twitter. There's a wealth of information available to help make Twitter a successful networking tool—far more than I can cover in this book on publishing—but the above suggestions should get you started. I highly recommend you do additional research on how Twitter can help gain exposure for you and your book. Place a Twitter link on your website, blog, Tumblr, Behance, or any and all of the other social media networking platforms you are using.

What more can you do to promote your book? Here's a fun one—book awards! You can find many opportunities to enter your book in award competitions. I have a list in the resources section of the book, but research it yourself. Make a master list of award competitions that are not only best suited for your book but also well-regarded. Take note of the submission requirements for each as well as the entry fees. Yes, there are entry fees. If you recall, we included $700 in our marketing budget for this, which means you should be able to enter approximately eight competitions.

Narrow it down to a price you can afford and record the dates on which those competitions will begin accepting submissions. Begin immediately if you can, and for those competitions you want to enter in the future, mark it on your calendar so that you don't miss out! Make a chart of each one, when you sent your book out, and when the judging will take place.

If you should place or win one (or more) of the competitions, the sponsors usually offer award stickers for you to purchase for your book cover. Order them; they won't be very expensive, and it's a real coup to not only be able to say your book is award-winning, but to be able to have your book speak for itself when you aren't there. If you have books in bookstores, take stickers there and put them on the book covers. Immediately create a press release and place it in the News section of your website. Place an announcement on your website homepage, create an email blast, update your blog, Tweet the news, and post on Facebook! This event should be used in all areas of your marketing and promotions.

*This is just for fun: a link that shows people buying books in real time all over the world!*

*www.bookdepository.com/live*

The sponsors of the awards competition will also be advertising the results. They will let you know whether it is in print or whether you will be able to attend a ceremony. Some will contact the finalists so they can travel to an event where the winners are announced in public. Don't miss out on that. It will be worth the experience regardless of the outcome.

If after all your submissions, you don't win an award, try not to be discouraged. The sponsors receive hundreds of books, and it can very difficult to narrow it down to a handful of winners. Some of the sponsors will email you feedback on how they judged your book. Read the feedback with an open mind. If it includes criticism that you truly feel doesn't apply, just let it go and don't look back. Take in what you feel might have a kernel of truth. It was worth the effort, and you can keep the comments in mind when you publish your next book—yes, your next book!

It's nearly impossible to cover everything in detail about publishing a photography book. So, if there is anything you wish I had included here, let me know by regular mail or through email on this book's website, and I'll try to include it on the book's blog and in the resource section online.

I sincerely hope this book proves to be a helpful resource for you in the publishing of your photography book. It's not an endeavor to take lightly—the demands on your time and energy are great, but they are very much worth it. Whether you sell ten or ten thousand copies, you've created something unique and valuable.

Your book will speak to people you cannot even imagine. Eventually your life will return to a sense of normalcy. Nothing stays the same; life is change. A year will pass, book signings will slow, perhaps there will be fewer speaking engagements, you'll have other responsibilities and opportunities to turn your attention to. You will go about your life, making breakfast, driving your mother to the doctor, going to work, watching a movie, eating a picnic lunch under that old tulip poplar.

Meanwhile, your book is still out there, traveling its own path. It will find its way into the hands of people you may never know, and it will change them in some small way. They will show it to someone they know; they will look through your photographs, read your words, and learn about you. It will make them feel something, think in a way they hadn't thought before, maybe challenge something they *had* thought, and it will change them too. Whether all of us realize it or not, we are extremely creative beings with our own ideas and visions about life, art, and nature. We teach each other through our actions, through our words, and through everything we create. And our creations inspire others. Congratulations on your book. Write to me, tell me about your book. I can't wait to see it!

94

# Resources

To the best of my knowledge, every resource listed here has been directly involved in some way, with photography and/or fine art books. Many I have had the good fortune to work with, and others have come highly recommended by people I trust. Always ask for samples of their work before hiring anyone and request quotes from no less than three. Finally, I suggest you have an in-depth meeting, in person or by phone, to determine who is the best fit to help you attain your unique vision in publishing your book. As of this printing, all of this contact information is correct, but nothing is static, so I plan to update these resources on this book's website regularly: www.HowtoPublishYourOwn PhotographyBook.com

---

## AWARDS

*Be sure to check submission requirements. Some of these only accept conventionally published books, some accept self-published books, most will only accept books printed offset, and others are for POD. Also, search the Web for awards that correspond with the theme of your book.*

THE ANNUAL INDEPENDENT PUBLISHER BOOK AWARDS (the IPPYs)
The Jenkins Group
Attn: Jim Barnes
1129 Woodmere Avenue, Suite B
Traverse City, Michigan 49686
www.independentpublisher.com/ipland/
IPAwards.php
1-800-707-4636, ext. 1011 (tel)

THE ARLES CONTEMPORARY BOOK AWARD
34 rue du docteur Fanton
13200 Arles, France
http://tinyurl.com/7faw7mh
www.rencontres-arles.com
33 (0)4 90 96 76 06 (tel)

BENJAMIN FRANKLIN BOOK AWARDS
Independent Book Publishers Association
627 Aviation Way
Manhattan Beach, CA 90266
http://ibpabenjaminfranklinawards.com/
310-372-2732 (tel)

THE DUMMY AWARDS
Festival Office
Koenigstor 14a
D-34117 Kassel, Germany
http://2011.fotobookfestival.org/en/dummy_
award/

THE EUROPEAN PUBLISHERS
AWARD FOR PHOTOGRAPHY
8, Broomfield Road, Heaton Moor, Stockport
SK4 4ND, England
http://tinyurl.com/7mxmyox
www.dewilewispublishing.com

THE GEORGE WITTENBORN AWARD
Attn: 2011 George Wittenborn Memorial
Book Award Committee
Rosemary Furtak / Library
Walker Art Center
1750 Hennepin Avenue
Minneapolis, MN 55403
http://tinyurl.com/34km7yn
www.arlisna.org/about/awards/wittenborn_info.html
612-624-1638 (tel)

PHOTOGRAPHY BOOK NOW
INTERNATIONAL JURIED COMPETITION
Blurb, Inc.
580 California Street, Suite 300
San Francisco, CA 94104
http://photographybooknow.blurb.com/

THE INTERNATIONAL BOOK AWARDS /
THE NATIONAL BEST BOOK AWARDS
9663 Santa Monica Blvd.
Suite 187
Beverly Hills, CA 90210
www.usabooknews.com
1-800-733-6511 (tel)

THE LOS ANGELES TIMES BOOK PRIZES
202 W. 1st Street
Los Angeles, CA 90012
http://events.latimes.com/bookprizes/
213-237-5000 (tel)

NAUTILUS BOOK AWARDS
Attn: Marilyn McGuire
P.O. Box 1359 (billing / mailing)
286 Enchanted Forest Road
Suite 102 A
Eastsound, WA 98245
marilyn@nautilusbookawards.com
www.nautilusbookawards.com

THE NEW YORK BOOK FESTIVAL
JM Northern Media LLC
7095 Hollywood Boulevard
Suite 864
Hollywood, CA 90028
www.newyorkbookfestival.com

THE NEXT GENERATION
INDIE BOOK AWARDS
511 Wilkinson Street
Chelsea, MI 48118
Info@IndieBookAwards.com
www.indiebookawards.com

PICTURES OF THE YEAR INTERNATIONAL
POYI: BEST PHOTOGRAPHY BOOK AWARD
Attn: Rick Shaw
315 Reynolds Journalism Institute
Columbia, MO 65211
www.poyi.org
573-884-2188 (tel)

PHOTO LUCIDA CRITICAL MASS BOOK AWARD
Box 3353
Portland OR 97208
http://tinyurl.com/7ka9bqr
www.photolucida.org
503-317-2083 (tel)

BOOK PRINTERS AND BINDERS

ASIA PACIFIC OFFSET
Ali M. Trujillo
1312 Q Street NW, Suite B
Washington DC 20009
www.asiapacificoffset.com
202-462-5436 (tel)

C&C OFFSET
Attn: Vicki Lundgren
PO Box 82037
Portland, OR 97282
www.ccoffset.com
503-233-1834 (tel)

CRAFTPRINT
9 Joo Koon Circle, Jurong
Singapore 629041
www.craftprint.com
(65) 6861 4040 (tel)

EDWARDS BROTHERS
380 Lexington Avenue
Suite 2902
New York, NY 10168
www.edwardsbrothers.com
212-867-2830 (tel)

FOUR COLOUR PRINT GROUP
Attn: Bekah Saylor
2410 Frankfort Avenue
Louisville, KY 40206
www.FourColour.com
502-896-9644

FRIESENS
One Printers Way
Altona, MB R0G 0B0, Canada
www.friesens.com/bookplant
204-324-6401 (tel)

IMAGO
http://www.imagousa.com/
Located in United States, South America, UK,
Europe, Australia, Hong Kong & China, Singapore, and India (see website for addresses and
telephone numbers at all locations)
212-921-4411 (tel) East Coast, Midwest,
and South America
949-367-1635 (tel) West Coast

MCNAUGHTON & GUNN, INC.
960 Woodland Drive

Saline, MI 48176
www.bookprinters.com
734-429-5411 (tel)

MM ARTBOOK PRINTING AND REPRO
1 rue Um Kläppchen
L - 5720 Aspelt
Luxembourg
marcel@mm-artbookprinting.com
http://tinyurl.com/85l4cws
00352 691.2009.30 (tel) and
Geleenstraat 68 B
6411 HT Heerlen
The Netherlands
0031 653.746.390 (tel)

ODDI PRINTING CORPORATION
Attn: Chuck Gershwin
chuck@oddi.com
215-885-5210
Iceland plant
Attn: Diana Sigurfinnsdottir
Hofdabakki 7
110 Reykjavik, Iceland
www.oddi.com

PACOM PACIFICA
Attn: Cecile Caronna
2133 Titan Street
Harvey, LA 70058
http://en.gopacom.com
504-362-3656 (tel)

PRINTING IN ITALY
99 The Embarcadero
San Francisco, CA 94105
www.PrintingInItaly.net
415-434-3331 (tel)

SHAPCO Printing
524 North 5th Street
Minneapolis, MN 55401
www.shapco.com
(612) 375-1150

## BOOK REPAIR AND CORRECTION SPECIALISTS

DUNN AND COMPANY
P.O. Box 1185
75 Green Street
Clinton, MA 01510
www.booktrauma.com
978-368-8505 (tel)

NUDEA CO. INC.
3813 Collins Lane
Louisville, KY 40245
www.nudea.net
502-327-8832 (tel)

## COLOR MANAGEMENT AND SCANNING

IOCOLOR
Attn: Gary Haukey
80 South Washington Street
Suite 200
Seattle, WA 98104
www.Iocolor.com
206-223-1845 (tel)

DEAN IMAGING
Attn: John Dean
2289 Forest Green Court

Marietta, GA 30062
www.deanimaging.com
404-270-9301 (tel)

DIGITAL PICTURE
1670 Northeast Expy. NE #C
Atlanta, GA 30329
www.digitalpicture.com
404-355-3400 (tel)

## DESIGN AND LAYOUT

HULAHOOP DESIGN
Attn: Sabine Beaupré
6912 Cedar Street
Wauwatosa, WI 53213
414-241-9388 (tel)

JILL DIBLE DESIGN
208 Overlook Drive
Woodstock, GA 30188
770-617-7704 (tel)

IAIN R. MORRIS
807 F Street
Petaluma, CA 94952
eyemorris@gmail.com
707-364-4087 (tel)

SHOCK DESIGN BOOKS
Attn: Laurie Shock
454 Hamilton Street SE, # 12
Atlanta, GA 30316
www.shockdesignbooks.com
770-312-7207 (tel)

## DESIGN, LAYOUT, BOOK DEVELOPMENT, AND PROJECT MANAGEMENT

BOOKHOUSE GROUP
Attn: Rob Levin
818 Marietta Street NW
Atlanta, Georgia 30318
www.bookhouse.net
404-885-9515 (tel)

JILL DIBLE DESIGN
208 Overlook Drive
Woodstock, GA 30188
770-617-7704 (tel)

SHOCK DESIGN BOOKS
Attn: Laurie Shock
454 Hamilton Street SE, # 12
Atlanta, GA 30316
www.shockdesignbooks.com
770-312-7207 (tel)

THE STORYLINE GROUP
Attn: Phil Bellury
1954 Airport Road, Suite 270
Atlanta, GA 30341
www.storylinegroup.com
770-458-1852 (tel)

## EDITORS AND PROOFREADERS

BAUMAN WORDSMITHS
Attn: Amy Bauman
2170 Leimert Boulevard
Oakland, CA 94602
510-482-8007 (tel)

CLARET COMMUNICATIONS
Attn: Julie Auton
1889 Castleway Lane NE
Atlanta, GA 30345
julietteauton@gmail.com
404-852-2167 (tel)

HOLLOWAY HOUSE
Attn: Shelley W. Holloway
2314 Briarcliff Commons NE
Atlanta, GA 30345
www.hollowayhouse.me

LAND ON DEMAND
Attn: Bob Land
20 Long Crescent Drive
Bristol, Virginia 24201
landondemand@bvunet.net

GINA WEBB
1803 Council Bluff Drive NE
Atlanta, GA 30345
404-315-4482 (tel)

DISTRIBUTORS,
FULFILLMENT HOUSES,
AND WHOLESALERS

APG SALES & DISTRIBUTION
7344 Cockrill Bend Boulevard
Nashville, TN 37209
www.apgbooks.com
800-327-5113 (tel)

BARNES AND NOBLE
*This is for order distribution through their stores.*
Small Press Department

122 Fifth Avenue
New York, NY 10011
http://tinyurl.com/3b7zq4

BAKER & TAYLOR
903 Pacific Avenue
www.btol.com
800-775-1800 (tel)

BOOK HUB
903 Pacific Avenue, #207A
Santa Cruz, CA 95060
www.book-hub.com
831-466-0145 (tel)

BOOK CLEARING HOUSE
46 Purdy Street
Harrison, NY 10528
www.bookch.com
800-356-9315 (tel)

CONSORTIUM
The Keg House
34 Thirteenth Avenue NE, Suite 101
Minneapolis, MN 55413-1007
www.cbsd.com
800-283-3572 (tel)

DISTRIBUTED ART PUBLISHERS (D.A.P.)
*D.A.P. is a distributor of art books in addition to
having their own small press, St. Ann's Press.
They represent publishers all over the world.*
155 Sixth Avenue, 2nd Floor
New York, NY 10013
www.artbook.com
212-627-1999 (tel)

FOTOFOLIO
561 Broadway
NY NY 10012
www.fotofolio.com

GREENLEAF BOOK GROUP
P.O. Box 91869
Austin, TX 78709
www.greenleafbookgroup.com
800-932-5420 (tel)

IDEA BOOKS
Nieuwe Herengracht 11
1011 RK  Amsterdam
The Netherlands
http://www.ideabooks.nl/
+31 20 6226154 (tel)

INDEPENDENT
PUBLISHERS GROUP
814 N. Franklin Avenue
Chicago, IL 60610
www.ipgbook.com
800-888-4741 (tel)

INGRAM BOOK COMPANY
1 Ingram Blvd.
La Vergne, TN 37086
www.ingrambook.com
800-937-8200 (tel)

PARTNERS PUBLISHERS GROUP
2325 Jarco Drive
Holt, MI 48842
www.partnerspublishersgroup.com
517-694-3205 (tel)

PERSEUS DISTRIBUTION
1094 Flex Drive
Jackson, TN 38301
www.perseusdistribution.com
800-283-3572 (tel)

PUBLISHERS GROUP WEST
1700 Fourth Street
Berkeley, CA 94710
www.pgw.com
800-788-3123 (tel)

SCB DISTRIBUTORS
15608 S New Century Drive
Gardena CA 90248
www.scbdistributors.com
800-729-6423 (tel)

SMALL PRESS UNITED
814 North Franklin Street
Chicago, IL 60610
http://smallpressunited.com
312-337-0747 (tel)

TEXTFIELD, INC.
4623 Collis Ave
Los Angeles CA 90032
http://www.textfield.org
213-784-3186 (tel)

## INDEPENDENT BOOK STORES

For a continually updated list of independent book stores, visit the resources section of this book's website: www.HowtoPublishYourOwn PhotographyBook.com.

## MARKETING AND PROMOTIONS

BCAUZ MARKETING
Attn: Terri Evans
Atlanta, GA
http://bcauz.com
404-593-8064 (tel)

JOHN KREMER BOOK MARKETING
P O Box 2887
Taos, NM 87571
http://www.bookmarket.com/consulting.htm
575-751-3398 (tel)

THE MATISSE GROUP
Attn: Mysty McLelland
Atlanta, GA 30309
mysty@thematissegroup.com
404-245-2246 (tel)

## MUSIC SOURCES FOR BOOK TRAILERS

ISTOCKPHOTO
ROYALTY FREE MUSIC
www.istockphoto.com/audio

Redbeard Music
www.redbeardmusic.com

Song Freedom
www.songfreedom.com

Triple Scoop Music
www.triplescoopmusic.com

## PHOTOGRAPHY BOOK GROUPS, EVENTS, AND LIBRARIES

ATLANTA CELEBRATES PHOTOGRAPHY
1135 Sheridan Road Northeast
Atlanta, GA 30324
www.acpinfo.org
404-634-8664 (tel)

FALL LINE PRESS PHOTO LIBRARY
1000 Marietta Street
Suite 112
Atlanta, GA 30318
www.FallLinePress.com

FLAK PHOTO
Andy Adams
1218 Rutledge Street #4
Madison, Wisconsin 53703
www.FlakPhoto.com

INDIE PHOTOBOOK LIBRARY
Larissa Leclair
1219 Blagden Alley, NW
Washington, DC 20001
www.indiephotobooklibrary.org

THE PHOTOBOOK CLUB
www.photobookclub.org

PHOTOBOOK LONDON
29-31 SAFFRON HILL
LONDON EC1N 8SW
www.photobookfair.co.uk
07880 735 269

## PHOTOGRAPHY BOOK AND OTHER BOOK GRANTS

**HONICKMAN FIRST BOOK PRIZE IN PHOTOGRAPHY**
Center for Documentary Studies at Duke
1317 W. Pettigrew Street
Durham, North Carolina, 27705
http://cds.aas.duke.edu/bp/index.html
919-660-3663 (tel)

**LIBRARY FELLOWS ARTIST BOOK GRANT**
National Museum of Women in the Arts
1250 New York Avenue, NW
Washington, DC 20005-3970
http://tinyurl.com/7ykcpdx
800-222-7270 (tel)

**PHOTO LUCIDA CRITICAL MASS BOOK AWARD**
Box 3353
Portland OR 97208
http://tinyurl.com/7ka9bqr
www.photolucida.org
503-317-2083 (tel)

## PHOTOGRAPHY GRANTS

*Your first stop for photography grants should be your city, county, and state local arts' grants associations. They will often fund photography projects, especially if they are regionally based. While these are not necessarily book grants, a book could be part of the project if you won the grant.*

**AARON SISKIND FOUNDATION**
c/o School of Visual Arts, MFA Photography
209 East 23rd Street
New York, NY 10010

www.aaronsiskind.org
http://grant.shootq.com/home
609-348-5650 (tel)

**ALEXIA FOUNDATION FOR WORLD PEACE ANNUAL PHOTOGRAPHY CONTEST**
www.alexiafoundation.org

**CAPELLI D'ANGELI FOUNDATION**
P.O. Box 305
Canton, CT 06019
www.capellidangelifoundation.org
860-693-6208 (tel)

**CHANGING IDEAS**
awards@changingideas.org
www.changingideas.org

**DOCUMENTARY PHOTOGRAPHY PROJECT DISTRIBUTION GRANTS**
Open Society Institute
400 West 59th Street
New York, NY 10019
yyamagata@sorosny.org
http://www.soros.org/grants
212-548-0600 (tel)

**FORWARD THINKING ARTIST AWARD**
info@forwardthinkingmuseum.com
http://www.forwardthinkingmuseum.com/contest/photography.php

**GUGGENHEIM FELLOWSHIPS**
John Simon Guggenheim
Memorial Foundation
90 Park Avenue
New York, NY 10016.
212-687-4470 (tel)

**THE ROSALYNN CARTER FELLOWSHIPS FOR MENTAL HEALTH JOURNALISM**
The Carter Center
One Copenhill
453 Freedom Parkway
Atlanta, GA 30307
http://www.cartercenter.org/health/mental_health/fellowships/index.html
800-550-3560 (tel)

**MICHAEL P. SMITH (MPS) FUND FOR DOCUMENTARY PHOTOGRAPHY**
New Orleans Photo Alliance
1111 St. Mary Street
New Orleans, LA 70130
http://www.neworleansphotoalliance.org/grants/MPS_Fund/index.php
504-610-4899 (tel)

**SHOOT Q GRANT**
http://grant.shootq.com/home

## PRINT-ON-DEMAND (POD) COMPANIES

*I am not endorsing any of the following companies. Do your own research and remember that some of these companies may charge fees (over and above simply printing the books) so study their terms closely. Also read the blog forums to learn about other people's experiences, and read the article on page 41 of this book: www.digitalhomethoughts.com/news/show/97676/0/1/15.*

**ADORAMAPIX**
www.adoramapix.com

**ASUKABOOK**
www.asukabook.com

Blurb
www.blurb.com

Infinity Publishing
www.infinitypublishing.com

Inkubook
inkubook.com

Lightning Source
www.lightningsource.com

Lulu
www.lulu.com

Kolo
www.kolo.com

Mpix
www.mpix.com

My Canvas
www.mycanvas.com

My Publisher
www.mypublisher.com

Photobook Canada
www.photobookcanada.com

Shutterfly
www.shutterfly.com

Unibook
www.unibook.com

Viovio
www.viovio.com

XLibris
www2.xlibris.com

## PROJECT MANAGEMENT

Deb Murphy
3393 Keswick Ct
Chamblee, GA  30341
debmurphy3@mac.com
404-405-5904 (tel)

Shock Design Books
Attn: Laurie Shock
454 Hamilton Street SE, Unit 12
Atlanta, GA 30316
www.shockdesignbooks.com
770-312-7207 (tel)

## PUBLICITY SPECIALISTS FOR BOOKS

BCauz Marketing
Attn: Terri Evans
Atlanta, GA
http://bcauz.com
404-593-8064 (tel)

The Matisse Group
Attn: Mysty McLelland
Atlanta, GA 30309
mysty@thematissegroup.com
404-245-2246 (tel)

Online Publicist
Attn: Lisa Roe
1852 North Fairwell Avenue, #1

Milwaukee, WI 53202
http://onlinepublicist.blogspot.com
onlinepublicist@gmail.com
414-243-2117 (tel)

Susan Schwartzman
Public Relations
www.susanschwartzmanpublicity.com
sjschwa@aol.com
877-833-4276 (tel)

Rose Carrano
Public Relations
151 W. 19th Street
Floor 3
New York, NY 10011
http://rosecarranopr.com
646-638-2181 (tel)

## PUBLISHING AGENTS

*While your best option may be approaching university and fine art presses where you don't need an agent, you will need one to represent you if you approach large publishing companies. Here are a select few agents who list photography books as part of their genre. Carefully review submission requirements before contacting them. You can research more agents on the Literary Marketplace website: www.literarymarketplace.com.*

Jennifer Lyons Literary Agency, LLC
Attn: Jennifer Lyons
151 West 19th Street, 3rd Floor
New York, NY 10011
www.jenniferlyonsliteraryagency.com
212-368-2812 (tel)

LEVINE GREENBERG LITERARY AGENCY
James A. Levine
307 Seventh Avenue, Suite 2407
New York, NY 10001
www.levinegreenberg.com
212-337-0934 (tel)

REGAL LITERARY INC.
Attn: Joseph Regal
The Capitol Building
236 West 26th Street, #801
New York, NY 10001
www.regal-literary.com
212-684-7900 (tel)

STERLING LORD LITERISTIC, INC.
Attn: Robert Guinsler
65 Bleecker Street
New York, NY 10012
www.sll.com
212-780-6050 (tel)

WAXMAN LITERARY AGENCY
Attn: Farley Chase
80 Fifth Avenue, Suite 1101
New York, NY 10011
www.waxmanagency.com
212-675-5556 (tel)


## PUBLISHING RELATED SERVICES

BOWKER
630 Central Avenue
New Providence, NJ 07974
www.bowker.com
877-310-7333 (tel)
888-269-5372 (tel)

LIBRARY OF CONGRESS
101 Independence Ave, SE
Washington, DC 20540
www.loc.gov/publish
202-707-5000 (tel)

U.S. COPYRIGHT OFFICE
101 Independence Avenue S.E.
Washington, D.C. 20559-6000
www.copyright.gov
202-707-3000 (tel)


## PUBLISHERS OF PHOTOGRAPHY AND FINE ART BOOKS

*Remember to check the submission guidelines carefully before contacting publishers. Take note of the companies that are not accepting unsolicited book proposals. This means you will have to find an agent to represent you for those particular publishers.*

5 CONTINENTS EDITIONS
Piazza Caiazzo 1
20124 Milano – Italia
www.fivecontinentseditions.com
+39 02 33603276 (tel)

21ST EDITIONS
9 New Venture Drive, #1
South Dennis, MA 02660
www.21stphotography.com
508-398-3000 (tel)

ABRAMS
115 West 18th Street, 6th Floor
New York, NY 10011
www.abramsbooks.com
212-206-7715 (tel)

ACTAR PUBLISHERS
151 Grand Street, 5th Floor
New York, NY 10013
www.actar.es
212-966-2207 (tel)
and
Roca i Batlle 2
08023 BARCELONA, Spain
+34 93 417 49 93 (tel)

AMMO BOOKS, LLC
300 S. Raymond Avenue
Suite 3
Pasadena, CA 91105
www.ammobooks.com
323-223-2666 (tel)

AMPHOTO BOOKS
Random House, Inc.
1745 Broadway
New York, NY 10019
www.randomhouse.com/crown/amphoto-books
212-782-9000 (tel)

APERTURE
547 W 27th Street, 4th Floor
New York, NY 10001
www.aperture.org
212-505-5555 (tel)

ASSOULINE
www.assouline.com
submissions@assouline.com
888-723-2099 (tel)

BALCONY PRESS
512 East Wilson Avenue, Suite 213
Glendale, California 91206

www.balconypress.com
818-956-5313 (tel)

CHRIS BOOT LTD
79 Arbuthnot Road
London SE14 5NP
www.chrisboot.com
+44 (0) 20 7639 2908 (tel)

CHRONICLE BOOKS
680 Second Street
San Francisco, California 94107
www.chroniclebooks.com
415-537-4200 (tel)

DA CAPO PRESS
Eleven Cambridge Center
Cambridge, MA 02142
www.perseusbooksgroup.com/dacapo/home.jsp
617-252-5200 (tel)

DISTRIBUTED ART PUBLISHERS (D.A.P.)
ST. ANN'S PRESS
155 Sixth Avenue, 2nd Floor
New York, NY 10013
www.artbook.com/stannspress.html
212-627-1999 (tel)

DAMIANI EDITORE
via Zanardi, 376
40131 Bologna, Italy
www.damianieditore.it
+39 051 6350805 (tel)

DEWI LEWIS PUBLISHING
8, Broomfield Road
Heaton Moor
Stockport SK4 4ND, England

www.dewilewispublishing.com
+44(0)161 442 9450 (tel)

EDITIONS BESSARD
12 rue de Rivoli
75004 Paris, France
www.editionsbessard.com

ÉDITIONS DIS VOIR
Danièle Rivière1 Cité Riverin
75010 Paris, France
www.disvoir.com
(33 - 1) 9 511 707 39 (tel)

FOTOFOLIO
561 Broadway
New York, NY 10012
www.fotofolio.com
submissions@fotofolio.com

GRAND CENTRAL PRESS
237 Park Avenue
New York, NY 10017
www.hachettebookgroup.com
grandcentralpublishing@hbgusa.com

GREYSTONE BOOKS
D&M Publishers
2323 Quebec Street, Suite 201
Vancouver, BC V5T 4S7
www.dmpibooks.com
800-667-6902 (tel)

THE ICE PLANT
Attn: Jacques Marlow
PO Box 29247
Los Angeles, CA 90029
www.theiceplant.cc

J&L BOOKS
PO Box 723991
Atlanta, GA 31139
www.jandlbooks.org
mail@JandLbooks.org

NAZRAELI PRESS
2871 NE Alameda Street
Portland, OR 97212
www.nazraeli.com
503-281-3621 (tel)

PANTHEON BOOKS
1745 Broadway
New York, NY 10019
http://pantheon.knopfdoubleday.com
212-782-9000 (tel)

PHAIDON PRESS LIMITED
Regent's Wharf
All Saints Street
London N1 9PA
www.phaidon.com
+ 44 20 7843 1000 (tel)

POWERHOUSE BOOKS
37 Main Street
Brooklyn, NY 11201
www.powerhousebooks.com
212-604-9074 (tel)

RADIUS BOOKS
1012 Marquez Place, Suite #109B
Santa Fe, NM 87505
www.radiusbooks.org
505-983-4068 (tel)

Rizzoli International
300 Park Ave South, 4th Floor
New York, NY 10010
http://www.rizzoliusa.com
212-387-3400 (tel)

Taschen
107 Greene Street
New York, NY 10012
www.taschen.com
212-226-2212 (tel)

Testify Books
305 West Broadway
Suite 233
New York, NY 10013
www.testifybooks.com
inquiries@testifybooks.com

Turner España
Rafael Calvo, 42 - 2º esc. izda.
28010. Madrid
www.turnerlibros.com
(+34) 91 3083336 (tel)

Twin Palms Publishers/TwelveTrees Press
54 1/2 East San Francisco Street
Santa Fe, New Mexico 87501 ·
www.twinpalms.com
800-797-0680 (tel)

Twin Lights Publishers, Inc.
8 Hale Street, Suite Two
Rockport, MA 01966
http://twinlightspub.com
978-546-7398 (tel)

## REVIEW SOURCES

*Here is a partial list of where to send your prepublication review copies four months prior to your book's publication date. Send them to your local newspapers and city magazines. and research other magazines that have a similar theme to the photography in your book. Some of these will have formal review submission requirements and specific mailing addresses, so go to their websites to review them before sending any packages.*

*If you can't find submission requirements, send an email and request them. These publications may have more than one reviewer, and they can come and go, so check the website to determine who the book reviewer is and send that person an email with your questions. I've included the names of those who are reviewers at the time of this book's publication.*

Aperture
547 W 27th Street, 4th Floor
New York, NY 10001
www.aperture.org

Chicago Sun-Times
350 N. Orleans Street, 10th Floor
Chicago IL 60654
Books: Teresa Budasi
tbudasi@suntimes.com
312-321-3000 (tel)
Chicago Tribune
435 N. Michigan Avenue, #400
Chicago IL 60611-4022
Books: Amy Guth
aguth@tribune.com
312-222-3232 (tel)

Christian Science Monitor
One Norway Street
Boston, MA 02115

Books: Marjorie Kehe
You have to email Ms. Kehe directly from the Christian Science Monitor's website.
617-450-2000 (tel)

ForeWord Magazine
Attn: Teresa Scollon
Book Review Editor
129 ½  East Front Street
Traverse City, MI 49684
www.forewordreviews.com/get-reviewed/submission-guidelines/
231-933-3699 (tel)

Kirkus Reviews
Independently published books:
www.kirkusreviews.com/indie/about

Lens Culture Photobook Review
Attn: Jim Casper
8 rue Saint Antoine
75004 Paris, France
http://www.lensculture.com/bookreview.html

Los Angeles Times Book Review
202 West 1st Street
Los Angeles CA 90012
www.latimes.com/features/books/
Attn: Susan Carpenter.
213-237-7778 (tel)

The Midwest Book Review
278 Orchard Drive
Oregon, WI 53575-1129
Editor-in-chief: James A. Cox
www.midwestbookreview.com/get_rev.htm
608-835-7937 (tel)

NEW YORK TIMES BOOK REVIEW
620 Eighth Avenue, 5th Floor
New York, NY 10018
Book reviewers: Michiko Kakutani, Janet
Maslin, and Dwight Garner
books@nytimes.com
www.nytimes.com/membercenter/faq/books.ht
ml#booksqa2

PUBLISHERS WEEKLY
Nonfiction Reviews
71 West 23 Street, #1608
New York, NY 10010
www.publishersweekly.com/pw/corp/
submissionguidelines.html

USA TODAY
7950 Jones Branch Drive
McLean, VA 22108
Attn: Carol Memmott
cmemmott@usatoday.com
703-854-3400 (tel)

*Send prepublication review copies as well as a
copy of your final book to:*

APOGEE PHOTO
Attn: Susan Harris
11121 Wolf Way
Westminster, CO 80031
www.apogeephoto.com

DIGITAL PHOTOPRO
Werner Publishing Corporation
12121 Wilshire Boulevard, 12th Floor
Los Angeles, CA 90025
www.digitalphotopro.com
310-820-1500 (tel)

EPHOTOZINE
Magezine Publishing Ltd
The Turbine
Shireoaks Triangle Business Park
Coach Close, Shireoaks
Nottinghamshire
S81 8AP, England
www.ephotozine.com

LENSWORK
Editor: Brooks Jensen
909 3rd Street
Anacortes, WA 98221
www.lenswork.com
360-588-1343 (tel)

PHOTO-EYE MAGAZINE / BOOKSTORE
Attn: Melanie McWhorter
370 Garcia Street
Santa Fe, NM 87501
www.photoeye.com
505-988-5152, ext. 112

OUTDOOR PHOTOGRAPHER
Werner Publishing Corporation
12121 Wilshire Boulevard
12th Floor
Los Angeles, CA 90025
www.outdoorphotographer.com
310-820-1500 (tel)

PHOTO DISTRICT NEWS
770 Broadway
7th Floor
New York, NY 10003
www.pdnonline.com
646-654-5780 (tel)

SHUTTERBUG
1415 Chaffee Drive, , Suite #10
Titusville, Fl USA 32780
www.shutterbug.com
editorial@shutterbug.com
321-269-3212 (tel)

## VIDEOGRAPHERS

*Here is a short list of videographers if you are looking
for professional help with your book trailer. Another
resource would be to find film students in your area.*

BASE CAMP MEDIA
Attn: Rich Addicks
www.basecampmedia.net
Atlanta, GA: 404-636-0925 (tel)
Big Sky, MT: 406-995-2087 (tel)

MARIA A. FLEET
1179 Rosewood Drive NE
Atlanta, GA 30306
678-641-7187 (tel)

JUMP\CUT PRODUCTIONS
Attn: Phil Walker
Atlanta, GA
www.Jumpcutpro.com
walkerp@me.com
404-408-2293 (tel)

ONE PRODUCTION PLACE
Attn: Neal Broffman
Atlanta, GA
www.oneproductionplace.com
neal@oneproductionplace.com
404-451-2462 (tel)

| Company | Color Book Quality with Sizes/Prices | Design Software and Templates | Accept PDF File of Your Design? | Printer Used and Color Specs | Paper Choices | Remove POD Logo Fr/Book | Online Bookstore Available For Use? |
|---|---|---|---|---|---|---|---|
| **Blurb**<br><br>*This pricing is for Blurb's standard books. They do offer a professional level called Pro-Line with higher quality paper and linen cover cloth, though the pricing is higher. Of all POD, I feel Blurb is the best quality at this time.* | Good printing with best binding. 21–40 pages minus shipping:<br>5 x 8 softcover starts $6.95<br>5 x 8 hardcover starts $21.95<br>6 x 9 softcover starts $8.95<br>6 x 9 hardcover starts $23.95<br>7 x 7 softcover starts $15.95<br>7 x 7 hardcover starts $25.95<br>8 x 10 softcover starts $22.95<br>8 x 10 hardcover starts $33.95<br>10 x 8 softcover starts $22.95<br>10 x 8 hardcover starts $33.95<br>13 x 11 hardcover starts $60.95<br>12 x 12 hardcover starts $65.95<br>(Blurb charges flat rate based on page range.) | 2 design options: Bookify, which is a simple online template program, and Booksmart, which you download to your computer to design your book. It offers many templates to choose from where you can mix and match pages and layouts. | Blurb offers a downloadable InDesign template to help you lay out your book. URL is www.blurb.com/make/pdf_to_book/template_indesign You can also use other third-party programs to design your book, but the PDF file must match their specifications. | HP Indigo Digital printer. Blurb accepts images saved as JPG and PNG. Blurb recommends you use sRGB for best color output or download Blurb's CMYK ICC color profile which is optimized for the printer they use. URL is: www.blurb.com/resources/color_management Files should be 300 dpi at size you want printed. | Standard–80#, Premium matte–100#, Premium Lustre–100#, ProLine Pearl Photo–140#, and ProLine Uncoated–100#. Price of book increases when you upgrade from standard paper. You can upgrade paper with any book. | Add 25% of cost of book. | Yes. You are paid monthly if your profits are $25 or more. If they are less, the profits roll over to the next month. To be paid by check, there is a $5 processing fee, but only a $1 processing fee if you use PayPal. |
| **Viovio**<br><br>*This pricing is for Viovio's standard books. They do offer a premium printed books with premium paper but they cost more.* | Good printing, but hard cover is not reinforced, and the gloss cover lamination is not as nice as Blurb's. For 30 pages minus shipping:<br>Softcover mini-book packs, various sizes, starts $19.99<br>9 x 7 softcover starts $13.99<br>9 x 7 hardcover starts $23.69<br>9.5 x 8 softcover starts $15.49<br>9.5 x 8 hardcover starts $25.49<br>11 x 8.5 softcover starts $25.99<br>11 x 8.5 hardcover starts $26.99<br>12.5 x 10 hardcover with a wire-o spine starts $37.99<br>14 x 11 softcover with a wire-o spine starts $27.00<br>8.5 x 8.5 softcover starts $13.99<br>8.5 x 8.5 hardcover starts $23.99<br>8.3 x 11.7 softcover starts $12.49<br>10 x 10 hardcover starts $26.99<br>12 x 12 softcover starts $36.49<br>12 x 12 hardcover starts $37.49<br>6 x 9 softcover starts $12.49<br>9 x 6 softcover starts $13.99<br>7 x 5 softcover starts $19.99<br>6.9 x 10.5 soft comic starts $12.49<br>8.5 x 11 softcover starts $12.49<br>8.5 x 11 hardcover starts $23.99<br>8 x 10 softcover starts $12.99<br>8 x 10 hardcover starts $23.99<br>13 x 11 hardcover starts $45.49<br>8 x 12 seamless layflat $106.88<br>(Viovio charges a base rate plus per-page.) | 2 design options: Viovio Book Designer and Viovio Book Machine. Viovio offers a few free templates where you can mix and match pgs. Also have many fee-based templates that range from .25 to $10. You can design your own template and sell it on their site for others to use. | Yes, but the PDF must match their specifications for correct output. They recommend you not use Scribus to create your book. | The Xerox iGen 3 is used for their Express Print and standard bks, which can cause a magenta cast. You may need to adjust for that. If you work in RGB, do not convert to CMYK and visa versa. Viovio prefers you use sRGB mode. Books are printed with a 7-color Electroink process. For this printer, use sRGB mode. All cover images should be sRGB mode. Files should be 300 dpi at size you want them printed. Viovio accepts file formats JPG, PNG, and GIF but prefers JPG to ensure best image quality. Avoid light color builds of less than 20% or you experience streaking. | Paper used is determined by the size and type of book you order. Sometimes you have an option; sometimes you do not. Papers include: Satin–80#, Digital Satin–80#, Digital Silk–100#, Photo Silk–100#, Text Futura–100#, Coated Gloss–120# | $10.00, plus $2.50 for each addit'l. if you order more than one book at a time. | Yes. You are paid 60 days after close of sale. To be paid by check sales must be $50 or more, and there is a $2.49 processing fee. To be paid by PayPal sales must be $25 or more and there may be a recipient fee depending on your type of PayPal acct. |

*Here are four POD companies with details on their photography book sizes, prices, design software, color management, and paper choices. These prices and specifications can change at any time. Go to this book's website for updated information on these companies. You should compare these variables with any POD company you consider working with.*

| Company | Color Book Quality with Sizes/Prices | Design Software and Templates | Accept PDF File of Your Design? | Printer Used and Color Specs | Paper Choices | Remove POD Logo Fr/Book | Online Bookstore Available For Use? |
|---|---|---|---|---|---|---|---|
| **MyPublisher**<br><br>*At the printing of this book, I have heard some photographers not as pleased with their books produced by My-Publisher. The problems were in the quality of the printing.* | Good printing, same level quality binding as Blurb, though hardcover laminate isn't as nice. Hardcover books have vellum fly sheets added to the front back of the inside book covers. Offering landscape books only:<br>3.5 x 2.75 mini book can only be 20 pages and costs $2.49<br>For 30 pages minus shipping:<br>7.75 x 5.75 Pocket softcover starts at $14.89<br>7.75 x 5.75 Pocket hardcover starts at $24.89<br>11.25 x 8.75 Classic hardcover starts at $39.89<br>15 x 11.5 Deluxe hardcover starts at $79.89<br>For super gloss paper/printing, add $10 per book to Classic hardcover bks up to 100 pgs. and $20 per book to Deluxe hardcover.<br>For new lay flat binding (up to 100 pages), add $10 per book for Pocket hardcover, add $20 per book for Classic hardcover, and add $40 per book for the Deluxe hardcover.<br>You have a large choice of covers such as linen and leather.<br>(MP charges a base rate plus per-page) | MyPublisher offers design software that you download to your computer with separate versions for Mac and PC. If you need help, templates are available but you also have the option to customize the design and layout of your pages. The file sizes can go as high as 900 MB, so be sure you have space and memory to manage them. | No. If you want even more design control than what MyPublisher offers with their software program templates, your only other option is to create full size page layouts in Adobe Photoshop or a similar image editing program and then save the individual pages as flattened JPG files that you can import into MyPublisher's software program just as you would a photo. | HP Indigo Digital printer. MyPublisher accepts images saved as JPG only. It's recommend you use sRGB or RGB for best color output. Their printer does not recognize gray-scale images so those too must be saved in RGB mode. Files should be 300 dpi at the size you want printed. | Mini books, Pocket and Classic hardcover books all print on a 115# gloss sheet. The Deluxe hardcover prints on 182# gloss sheet. You can also pay extra if you want your Classic or Deluxe hardcover books printed on the new Super Gloss paper. | $10 per book. | No |
| **Shutterfly** | Okay quality printing. I would not recommend for high-end art or photography books. Landscape or square books only.<br>For 30 pages minus shipping:<br>7 x 5 softcover starts $17.99<br>9 x 7 softcover starts $20.99<br>8 x 8 softcover starts $29.99<br>8 x 8 hardcover starts $39.99<br>8 x 8 leather die cut starts $49.99<br>11 x 8 softcover starts $34.99<br>11 x 8 hardcover starts $44.99<br>11 x 8 leather die cut starts $54.99<br>12 x 12 hardcover starts $69.99<br>12 x 12 leather die cut starts $84.99<br>(Shutterfly charges a base rate plus per-page) | 2 design options: Simple Path and a Custom Path system. With Simple Path, you upload your images and Shutterfly instantly creates your book by arranging the photos chronologically with 20 pre-set backgrounds to choose from. With Custom Path, you have creative control moving pictures and text in addition to having access to backgrounds, layouts, and embellishments. | No. If you want more design control than what is offered with Shutterfly's software program templates, your only other option is to create full-size page layouts in Adobe Photoshop or a similar image editing program and then save the individual pages as flattened JPG files that you can import into Shutterfly's software program just as you would a photo. | Fuji Frontier Digital printer. Shutterfly accepts images saved as JPG only. It's recommend you use sRGB for best color output. Files should be 300 dpi at the size you want printed. | 100# gloss | There is no option at this time to print your book without the Shutterfly logo. | No |

*Prices, options, and terms for these companies can change at any time.*

©2012 Shock Design Books
www.shockdesignbooks.com
www.howtopublishyourownphotographybook.com

*Note: With all of these, there are additional options to choose from such as die-cut covers, book jackets, and other finishings which may change the price of the book.*

# Glossary

**A**

ACKNOWLEDGMENTS: Typically one page in length, this is where the author thanks specific people who were helpful in completing the book. It can appear in the front matter of a book or in the back matter.

ADOBE CREATIVE SUITE: A software bundle package from Adobe that includes Acrobat, Illustrator, InDesign, and Photoshop.

ADOBE INDESIGN: A software program used to design and lay out books and publications.

ADOBE PHOTOSHOP LIGHTROOM: A software program used with Adobe Photoshop for image management, editing, and processing.

ADVANCE COPY also known as pre-publication review copy: Bound pages of a book before it has been proofread and printed. This is used as a marketing tool and sent to reviewers approximately four months prior to the book's publication date.

AGENT (Literary agent): A person who represents you and your work to book publishers.

AQUEOUS COATING: A water-based protective coating applied on press to protect the printed surface of your book jacket or brochure. It provides more protection than a varnish but less than a laminate or UV coating.

**B**

BACK MATTER: Pages in the back of a book that can include an Afterword, Artist Statement, Author bio, Acknowledgments, Appendices, and Colophon.

BLUELINE PROOF (see also ozalids): Inexpensively produced proofs of a book that, traditionally, have been printed on light-sensitive paper producing a blue color. The proofs show text and photography in position with gathered or stapled sections and trim marks. The paper does not reflect what the book will print on.

BOOK PACKAGER: One who provides the services of editing, design, layout, and printing/binding for a publisher, corporation, or individual. Some packagers will also develop and produce their own book concepts and sell them to a publisher.

BOOK TRAILER: A multi-media or video advertisement for a book.

BOOKLAND EAN BARCODE: A scannable barcode that incorporates the publisher's ISBN number and the country where the book is being sold. This barcode differs from regular barcodes in that it has a five-digit extension that reveals the price of the book.

BOOKS IN PRINT: A resource for bookstores and libraries, this is a searchable database of all books available for sale in the United States, compiled by the company Bowker. To be included, the book must have an ISBN.

BOWKER: Publisher of Books in Print, Bowker is the official U.S. ISBN Agency and collects bibliographic information on published books and periodicals.

BOWKERLINK: An automated tool enabling publishers to manage their books, ISBNs, barcodes, and registration information online.

**C**

CASE: The cloth- or paper-covered boards that make up a hard cover book.

CATALOGING IN PUBLICATION (CIP) DATA: A bibliographic record for a book that is compiled by the Library of Congress before it is published. The data is used as a resource for booksellers and librarians.

CHICAGO MANUAL OF STYLE (CMS) A style guide of American English that is the preference for use in editing books.

CMYK: An abbreviation for inks used in 4/color process offset printing: cyan, magenta, yellow, and black.

COLOPHON (see also copyright page): Typically placed in the back of a book, this contains copyright, ISBN, production, and publishing information about the book. When the information is placed in the front of the book, it's normally called a copyright page.

COLOR MANAGEMENT: Maintaining quality and consistency of color from scanning a transparency or negative, to processing and viewing the image on your computer screen, and printing the images on press.

COLOR SPACE: The range of colors available within a specific color group, such as RGB or CMYK.

COMB BINDING: Rectangular holes are punched into the pages of a book and plastic spines are inserted into the holes, thus binding the pages.

CONTINUOUS TONE: An image in which the colors and shades blend seamlessly into one another without a pattern. A traditionally printed photograph is an example of continuous tone.

CONVENTIONAL PUBLISHER: A conventional publisher owns the

publishing rights to a book and controls and underwrites the editing, design, production, and distribution. The author retains copyright to the work and is paid a percentage of the net sales.

COPYEDIT: To edit and correct written materials for spelling, grammar, and punctuation.

COPYRIGHT PAGE (see also Colophon): Typically placed on the reverse side of a title page, this contains copyright, ISBN, production, and publishing information about the book. When the information is placed in the back of the book, it's normally called a colophon.

CROWDSOURCED FUNDING: A platform that brings together proposed projects and social media exposure to millions of people who can collectively financially support the endeavor in small or large amounts.

**D**

DEBOSSING: The application of heat and great pressure to create a recessed impression in the cloth or paper of a book case or book jacket. Book titles, graphic elements, and logos are examples of what might be debossed.

DIGITAL PRINTING: The process of printing an image digitally, with-out printing plates, using pigment or toner.

DISTRIBUTOR: A company that represents you and your book to booksellers using marketing materials. A distributor also warehouses your books and processes orders.

DUOTONE: A halftone reproduction of an image using two specific spot colors to create depth within the picture. A tritone uses three inks, and a quadtone uses four.

**E**

EBOOK: A digital version of a book that can be viewed on computers, electronic reading devices, or smartphones.

EMBOSSING: The application of heat and great pressure to create a raised impression in the cloth or paper of a book case or book jacket. Book titles and logos are examples of what might be embossed.

ENDPAPERS OR ENDSHEETS: Paper that is glued to the inside of the hardcover case boards and attached to the pages of the body of a book. In some cases, they are also reinforced with cloth for durability.

EPUB: An ebook format that allows for reflowable content enabling the reader to adjust the size of the text for readability.

**F**

F&Gs: An abbreviation for folded and gathered sheets, these are printed pages of a book that have been folded down into sections and trimmed. They are sent to the publisher/author for approval before the printer sews and binds the book.

FLEXBIND: A method of smyth-sewn book binding that is softcover with endpapers and flaps. It's a hybrid between a typical softcover and hardcover book. This book has a flexbound binding.

FM SCREENING (see also stochastic screening): This stands for "frequency modulation" which simulates continuous tone in offset printing. It uses dots like halftones, but these dots are much smaller and positioned in a dithering pattern for smoother gradations.

FOIL STAMP: A print process that uses heat and pigment or metallic foil to stamp an impression onto a paper or cloth surface. This is a typical finishing effect used on book cases and jackets.

FOREWORD: An essay or remarks about the book, written by someone other than the author.

FRENCH-FOLD JACKET: A book jacket with folds at the top and the bottom. These are typical on large size books where if a standard book jacket were used, it would be subject to curling with wear.

FULFILLMENT HOUSE: This is a company that warehouses your books and process orders, but does no marketing or promotions of your book.

FRONT MATTER: Pages in the front of a book that can include title pages, copyright page, dedication, acknowledgments, table of contents, preface, foreword, and introduction.

**G**

GAMUT: The range of color that can be represented while using a specific color space on a certain output or viewing device.

**H**

HALFTONE: A printing technique that reproduces a continuous-tone image using a series of dots that vary in size and shape, and each ink's halftone dot is printed at a specific angle.

HEADBAND: A strip of woven threads around a string or cane center that is attached to a cotton tape. Sometimes it's sewn into the top and bottom of a book binding, reducing strain on the spine and other times it's glued in as a decorative element.

**I**

ICC Color Profile: A file containing data characterizing the color of a specific device such as a camera, scanner, or a printing press, according to standards set by the International Color Consortium (ICC).

Introduction: An essay in the front matter that can be written by the author or by someone knowledgeable on the subject of the book.

ISBN: An abbreviation for international standard book number, the ISBN is a thirteen-digit number code registered to a specific book that identifies it to book buyers.

**J**

Jacket: A printed paper that wraps around a hard-cover book. It contains the title of the book, the author, descriptive text, photographs or art, and a bookland EAN barcode. As a marketing piece, it is usually highly designed in order to attract attention and garner sales. It also serves as a protective covering over the hard- cover case.

**L**

Lamination: A matte or glossy film that is applied to a book case or jacket using a wet or thermal method. The films come in different thicknesses and create a very durable surface.

Library of Congress: The national library of the United States and a research library that can be used by the public. It holds approximately 147 million items and 33 million books.

Liftgate: A lifting platform at the rear of a truck to enable the loading and unloading of cargo when a loading dock is not present.

Limpbound: A term used mainly with printers in Asia, it's a softcover binding that is smyth sewn for durability rather than glued.

LMP: An abbreviation for the "Literary MarketPlace," The LMP is both a book and an online database of agents listing their specific genres of representation to publishing companies, status of submissions, and contact information.

**O**

Offset printing (lithography): A printing method where imagery on an inked plate is transferred to a rubber blanket, and then to paper. The plates are dampened with water rollers, and the ink is distributed to the image areas of the plate. The oil-and-water-do-not-mix formula keeps inked areas crisp.

Ozalids (see also blueline proofs): A name used in Great Britain for blueline proofs.

**P**

Pallet jack (pallet truck): A tool that will lift and move pallets when a loading dock is not present.

PMS: An abbreviation for the "Pantone Matching System," which is a color guide containing thousands of colors. Each one has an specific number representing a custom ink for use in offset printing.

Perfect Bound: A method of book binding in which the edges of the pages are roughed up and then glue is applied to bind the book block to the softcover. While it is a less-expensive method, it is not as durable as a sewn binding.

PCN: An abbreviation for "preassigned control number," this is a unique numerical identifier for books prior to being published. It enables the book to be searchable with librarians. A publisher with more than ten books published can move from the PCN program to the CIP data program which is more comprehensive.

PDF: An abbreviation for "portable document format," this is a file format that captures the look and elements of a page or series of pages, and allows the page to be viewed by others who don't have the program the file was created in. It's also a method of creating an ebook with a fixed layout that is viewable on computers, an iPad, and iPhone.

POD: An abbreviation for "print-on-demand," this is a digital method of printing and binding a book, one copy at a time.

Preface: Typically this is the author's statement about the book, though increasingly, it's also being used as a place to print a statement written by others.

Prepress: The various production steps that must be completed to prepare a book before it goes to press. This can include applying ICC color profiles to digital images, producing prepress proofs, and preflighting the document to ensure there are no missing graphics, fonts, or other issues that could compromise outputting the file to plates.

Press kit: Also called a media kit, this is a package that should be sent to the media, in advance of the book's publishing, to announce the book and provide information about both it and the author.

Printed litho case: This is a hard cover book that has a color printed cover resembling a book jacket except that it is glued to the boards, and there are no flaps.

PROCESS COLOR: Also known as four color (4/c), this refers to CMYK inks used in offset printing.

PROOFREAD: This is the read, done by an editor, when the book is in its final form before going to press. The editor looks for errors in layout or text and makes sure everything conforms, as much as possible, to the *Chicago Manual of Style*.

Q

QR CODE: An abbreviation for "quick response code," it's a matrix barcode that is linked to a URL, video, or audio and accessed by scanning with a smartphone QR code reader.

QUARKXPRESS: A graphic design software program used to design and lay out books and publications.

R

RGB: An abbreviation for "red, green, blue," this term refers to the additive colors of light as viewed on a computer monitor .

ROYALTY: A payment to an author by a publisher based on a percentage of net sales.

RSS/ATOM FEED: A format for de-livering regularly changing Web content.

S

SELF-PUBLISHING: Publishing your own book without the imprint, services, or underwriting of a pub-lishing company.

SIDE-SEWN BINDING: A method of binding where the book block is sewn on the side, approximately 1/4" in from the spine of the book. It's the most durable binding method, but the pages will not lay flat.

SIGNATURE: A large sheet of paper with multiple pages printed on both sides. Quite often a signature has 16 pages, but signatures can also be 4-, 6-, 8-, 10-, or 12-pages. The pages are then folded down and trimmed into sections that are sewn into a book.

SMYTH-SEWN BINDING: The sig-nature sections of the printed pages are sewn together with binding thread at the folds, creat-ing durability yet also allowing the pages to lay flat.

SPIRAL BINDING: Sometimes called coil binding, this is a method where round or oval holes are punched through the edges of the pages allowing a spiral plastic coil to be woven through the holes

STOCHASTIC SCREENING: Also known as FM screening, which stands for "frequency modulation," this system uses dots just as halftone screening does, but the dots used in this process are smaller. The dots also differ in that halftone dots vary in size, while these dots remain the same size. In this system, the dots are positioned similar to a dithering pattern that mimics continuous tone. Four Colour Print Group uses a hybrid process of this called Sublima.

SUBSIDY PUBLISHER Authors pay for the production of their books with these publishers, who can be selective about which books they publish. They contribute editing, proofreading, and other services to prepare the book to sell. While the author usually owns the copy-right to the work, the publisher owns publishing rights as well as the books and holds possession of them until they sell and the author receives royalty payments.

T

TRIM SIZE: This refers to the page size of a book, not the size of a cover, which can be larger.

U

UV COATING: A clear glossy liquid applied to paper and then cured with ultraviolet light. It can be ap-plied over the entire sheet or in spot areas. It is a highly protective finish.

V

VANITY PUBLISHER: This is a com-pany that will take your book and publish it completely at your ex-pense. A vanity publisher does not screen for quality and will publish anything. The author retains copy-right, takes possession of the books, and receives all profits from any book sales. The publisher does no marketing or distribution.

W

WET PROOF: A series of pages from a book printed on press for the purpose of testing color before printing the entire book. This is an affordable option with books printed in Asia, but not for those published in the United States.

WHOLESALER: This is a company that buys books directly from pub-lishers at an even steeper discount than bookstores do—55 to 65 per-cent off the list price of the book. Wholesalers stock the books in warehouses and sell them to stores at a low discount and then pocket the difference. They don't repre-sent the authors; they represent the stores to whom they sell. Wholesalers will buy from pub-lishing companies but not neces-sarily from a self-published author.

## ABOUT THE AUTHOR

President of Shock Design Books, Laurie Shock has designed and produced over two hundred books, including *A Century of Women* with Turner Broadcasting, and *Isaac Asimov's Library of the Universe*. Her client list includes the American Cancer Society, The Centers for Disease Control and Prevention, The Carter Center, Longstreet Press, Peachtree Publishers, Shepherd Center, and Vineyard Stories. Many of the books she has designed and produced have been published internationally, including a cancer memoir published in Japan. Three of her books have won international book awards.

She co-produced the traveling exhibit, "Blind/Sight: Conversations with the Visually Inspired," creating illustrations of how each person in the exhibit sees, based on in-depth interviews and guidance from each subject.

She has taught publishing workshops for Atlanta Celebrates Photography with the Showcase School, at Turner Broadcasting System, and at Serenbe Photography Center.

Her current book projects include a photography monograph by Kael Alford, *Bottom of da Boot: Louisiana's Disappearing Coast* and *America 101*, photographs by Arthur Grace. Both books are for Fall Line Press to accompany the photographers' exhibits at the High Museum of Art in Atlanta, Georgia. She lives in Atlanta with her husband, Billy Howard, and their really big cat, Sam.

## ABOUT THE PHOTOGRAPHER

Billy Howard is a documentary photographer specializing in public health and education. His photographic books include *Epitaphs for the Living: Words and Images in the Time of AIDS*; *Portrait of Spirit: One Story at a Time*, with an introduction by Christopher Reeve; and *Angels and Monsters: A Child's Eye View of Cancer* for The American Cancer Society.

WITHDRAWN

He co-produced the exhibit "Blind/Sight: Conversations with the Visually Inspired," creating large format photographic portraits accompanied by interviews of visually impaired participants. It is currently on display in Atlanta and Minneapolis.

His work has been featured on *Good Morning America*, *CBS This Morning*, NPR's *Performance Today*, and in the HBO special *The Coming Plague*. His work was projected in the Olympic stadium during the opening ceremonies for the 1996 Summer Olympic Games in Atlanta, Georgia.

The Smithsonian Institution included his images documenting the AIDS crisis in their 2012 Folklife Festival on the National Mall in Washington DC.

Howard is a 2011–2012 Rosalynn Carter Fellow in Mental Health Journalism, and holds an honorary doctor of literature degree from St. Andrews College in Laurinburg, North Carolina. He lives in Atlanta with his wife, Laurie Shock, and their really big cat, Sam.

YALE

Front cover: I was hiking into a remote farming village in Bangladesh, and just as it started to rain, I came around a bend in the trail and discovered a girl from the village bathing in the pond.

 I traveled up the Brahmaputra River in this country boat. One of the crew was pushing off from a small island, called a char, that we visited.

 Covering the first Palestinian elections, I took a break and visited Rachel's tomb on the outskirts of Bethlehem.

 Despite crushing poverty, this young mother in a slum in New Delhi dressed in beautifully colored cloth.

 In the mountains of Nicaragua, we stopped at a small farm. This girl, peeking from the shed used for cooking, was curious about her new guests.

 Elmina is a fishing village on the coast of Ghana and one of the most stunning places I have visited.

 Leaving a small community in Bangladesh, the local kids followed us out, scampered up this tree, and waved farewell.

 A one-room school in Changeshu village, a remote area in northern Ghana.

 After a day of sightseeing, this young tourist and his bird take a break in Oaxaca, Mexico.

 A member of a family circus poses before a performance in Isla Mujeres, Mexico.

 Pretty girls in their pretty dresses walk down the road, checking out the photographer behind them in Bangladesh.

 Above a crater lake in Nicaragua, a group of nuns takes a break to see the sights.

 A young girl fighting guinea worm disease in Ghana.

 On a hot day in the Hugo Chavez barrio outside Managua, Nicaragua, a young girl finds a way to cool off.

 After clamoring off a school bus, a young girl in Kyoto flashes a peace sign at a photographer, to the delight of her companions.

 Back cover: Most photographers I know, hate having their photograph taken. Here I am getting a dose of my own medicine from photographer, Pam Drake.

*ABOUT THE PHOTOGRAPHS*
*by Billy Howard*

# ACKNOWLEDGMENTS

This labor of love involved a lot of help from some very generous and supportive people.

Thank you, Kathryn Kolb, for convincing me there was a need for this book in the first place. Without you I would not have begun teaching the workshops that led to the writing of this book.

To my students at Serenbe—Anne Berry, Chet Burgess, Diane Fox, Tamara Gehle, Judy Lampert, Ronald Nuse, Hettie Summerlin—Thank you for inspiring me as we brainstormed and planned your books. I hope you will all share them with me when you publish them.

To John Yow, my first friend and colleague upon arriving in Atlanta in 1991. Thank you for reading my book, suggesting wonderful changes, and always being my dear friend.

Marilyn Suriani and Bill Smith: Thank you for reading my book in its early stages and offering great feedback to encourage me. And, Marilyn, I so appreciate your willingness to be interviewed to share your story of publishing and your stunning documentary photography.

To Ellen Fleurov, a dear friend and gifted photography historian and museum curator. Thank you for your unconditional support both personally and professionally.

To Eliot Dudik whom I met at the ACP Book Fair last year where I fell in love with your book. Thank you for being a part of this and offering your publishing experience to photographers who will benefit from your photography book publishing endeavors.

To Kaylinn Gilstrap and Neil Broffman. Thank you both for helping me take the first steps into the world of video and multimedia—a whole new world of storytelling.

Thank you, Kelbi McCumber, for assisting me in my publishing workshop and for all of your encouraging support that this might be of use to others.

Harris Fogel: Thank you for reading my book, for your invaluable contributions and suggestions, and for your continuing friendship and support.

Deep gratitude to my dear friend and editor Amy Bauman—we have great history together in publishing, going back many years. Those early memories are so rich, and I feel very fortunate that we continue to work together today.

Alison Shaw, I truly admire you and your work and am grateful to you for writing the foreword to this book.

Finally to my husband, Billy, whose photographs make this book so beautiful: Thank you for putting up with the long hours I've spent writing this, for your smart editorial suggestions, and for your ever wise counsel. You are my partner in everything.

# INDEX